Risk Wise

Nine everyday adventures

Polly Morland

Photographs by Richard Baker

Published in association with
The School of Life

THE
SCHOOL
OF LIFE

P

PROFILE BOOKS

First published in Great Britain in 2015 by
Profile Books Ltd
3 Holford Yard
Bevin Way
London WC1X 9HD
www.profilebooks.com

Published in association with
The School of Life
70 Marchmont Street
London WC1N 1AB
www.theschooloflife.com

All photographs reproduced by permission: page 20, © NASA/
Chris Hadfield; page 102 © Marcus Hartmann 2013/www.photo-
hartmann.de; page 128, © Christian Schuh; page 130, © ICRC/
Kate Holt. All other photographs © Richard Baker 2015.

A CIP catalogue record for this book is available from the
British Library.

ISBN 978 1 78125 448 6
eISBN 978 1 78283 156 3

All reasonable efforts have been made to obtain copyright
permissions where required. Any omissions and errors of
attribution are unintentional and will, if notified in writing to the
publisher, be corrected in future printings.

Text design by sue@lambledesign.demon.co.uk
Typeset in Dante by MacGuru Ltd *info@macguru.org.uk*

Printed and bound in Britain by Bell & Bain Ltd

MIX
Paper from
responsible sources
FSC® C007785

For my mother:
'Is that wise?'

Contents

Introduction

The original plan was to open this book with a bold utopian vision of a world without risk, a carefree El Dorado where nothing that we hold dear is suffered to hang in any kind of infernal balance, but instead is suspended in a bubble of immaculate and infinite safety. The transported reader would be reminded of the finer sort of science fiction or perhaps one of those elegant thought experiments beloved of late twentieth-century bluestockings. The graceful conceit would then set the stage for a timely and orderly meditation upon risk in the modern world.

It would have been great, if only it had worked.

But instead the utopia quickly turned into dystopia and from there into chaos – not, one hopes, because of the ineptitude of the writer, but because of the sheer impossibility of removing the notion of risk from any imaginable form of human life. Please, feel free, try it yourselves and good luck, but do not expect a smooth ride.

For quite apart from the troublesome business of mortality, which – you have been warned – is a serious obstacle for anyone foolhardy enough to hallucinate a risk-free existence, there also remains the sticky issue of how fundamental risk is to our temporal day-to-day lives. It is because we do not know what is going to happen and we mind about what does that the notion of risk exists at all.

Yet something strange has happened to it in recent years. So cosseted from many sorts of danger have we in the developed world become that we have rather lost our bottle; or at least we think we have, which in itself can be curiously self-fulfilling. We hark back to an age when the sorrows and misfortunes of earlier generations were simply absorbed by doughty folk hardened to disaster and disappointment. And our nostalgia for their bygone resilience, although we in part invented it to fit our story, means that we tend not to see their travails and their triumphs through the prism of risk. No, rather in the way that teenagers with spots and broken hearts feel that their anguish surpasses any prior heartache, so we in the modern world feel that we *own* risk somehow, that our experience of it is uniquely intense. Moreover, because our secular society has replaced divine ordinance with a cult of individual control, we read our whole lives through a balance sheet of risks and safeguards, so that when anything goes wrong, as it inevitably does, we reflexively hunt for the person who should have seen it coming all along (this is called the hindsight bias, more of which later on).

The crux is this: in one sense the urge towards safety can be, and is, good; but if left unchecked, it fosters a delusional zeal to stamp out every last pernicious risk where'er it lurks, fudging the neutral idea of uncertainty with the negative one of hazard. Indeed, your thesaurus will tell you that

'hazard' and 'risk' are one and the same, but do not be fooled; they are not. And, if this book sets out to do one thing, it is to disabuse you of that.

What if we were to look beyond an idea of risk conjured alone by TV images of planes hitting skyscrapers, bankers slumped on desks as stocks flat-line or of lone polar bears teetering on shrinking icebergs? What if we were to entertain the thought that sometimes risk can be good? Whisper it, for in your heart you already know that we each of us take a thousand large or small risks every day. When you cross the road, get on the train, climb a hill, hurry downstairs, voice an opinion, tell a white lie, butter some toast, drink a beer, say a prayer, take a holiday, take a job, lean in for a kiss, slam a door in rage, buy a house, buy a book, say goodbye, say hello, each of these acts contains a few essential particles of risk. And could the time have finally come to celebrate the fact?

Peruse, with an eye to risk, the corpus of ancient Greek ethics and you quickly realise much of it is given over to contemplation of the essential ingredients of risk: how much of human life depends upon things, both good and bad, that humans cannot control and how the good man (or woman) can reasonably be expected to navigate the fact. Aristotle in particular spent a lifetime teasing out ideas of a good life that is only meaningful as pursued in a world where it is not necessarily handed to you on a plate. Indeed, the heart of his ethics turns on the idea of the 'Golden Mean'; that the virtues live in some state of equilibrium with their concomitant vices, so courage sits at the halfway point between rashness and cowardice, generosity between extravagance and meanness, modesty between shyness and shamelessness and so on.

Risk was not isolated for this treatment, of course. Aristotle was a millennium and a half too early for that – and besides it is not a virtue – but this book proposes that we nevertheless borrow the philosopher's model. Given that a world without risk is unthinkable and that hyper-caution may prove as undesirable, and as hazardous, as mindless thrill-seeking, consider this: where with regard to risk might the Golden Mean lie? Where is the Risk Wise sweet spot?

The point is that there are evidently people out there who know, or who have learned, how to live with risk in intelligent, enriching ways; there are people out there who are risk wise. This is their book. It is about what they feel and how they think.

And whether indeed the rest of us might learn to be risk wise too. In the words of intelligent risk-takers everywhere, *why not?*

1

Playing with fire

A small girl is hammering a four-inch nail into a plank of wood. She wears a pink sundress and black school shoes without socks. She is concentrating intensely, hammering hard. The steel shaft of the nail is gripped between grubby finger and thumb, the plank itself balanced precariously against a short section of concrete sewer pipe, on which someone has spray-painted a few squiggles. One swing of the hammer, a rubber-handled DIY-store affair, glances off the side of the little girl's thumb. She pulls a face and squeezes the thumb into her palm for a moment. Then she resumes pounding away until a tiny curlicue of wood appears on the other side of the plank, chased by the shiny point of the nail.

'I'm making something,' she says, without looking up, and grabs a rusty-looking saw from the ground by her feet.

Passing a charred fire-pit where some kids lit a blaze the day before, two cousins scramble to the summit of a great, honeycombed heap of wooden pallets. They take it in turns to leap off the highest point onto the fibreglass prow of an old boat beneath. Airborne, they pedal the sunshine for a few seconds before landing with a whoop and a sound like a distant explosion.

'It makes you bounce,' yells one to the other.

It does not look safe, this boat crash pad, but it does look fun. So much fun, in fact, you find yourself wondering whether they might let you have a go.

Not far away is a trickle of a stream, full of what appears to be rubbish – more tyres, a single red shoe, an industrial cable spool, some grey upholstery foam and an old metal school chair with no seat. The stream is flanked by tall trees, where a girl and a boy are climbing in their bare feet.

'Does Mum know I'm out?' one of them asks the other.

'I don't know,' comes the reply, and they keep climbing.

★ ★ ★

This pied piper of a junkyard can be found tucked away down an alley behind a drab community building in the centre of Plas Madoc, a housing estate south of Wrexham in North Wales. Plas Madoc is in the top 10 per cent of the Welsh Index of Multiple Deprivation. It is not for nothing that people round here call it Smack Madoc or Cardboard City. Ever since the estate was built in the sixties, local children have played on this acre or so of wasteland, carved in two by a brook that dwindles in summer, gushes in winter. Though it is little more than a puddle on this hot summer's day, there were stories years ago that a child had drowned in it, long before the estate was built. Locals here

recollect their mothers saying to them as children, 'You've not been down at the brook, have you?', to which they would shake their heads – lying – 'No, absolutely not.'

But the children of Plas Madoc loved this scraggy plot of nothingness between houses. It was their space, their 'room of one's own'. They called it simply The Land. No one round here can ever remember it being called anything else.

In recent years, this kind of play – free, unsupervised, prone to scrapes and bumps, sometimes unkind, often daft and almost always dirty – has been deemed to be in crisis. A generation of children, so we are told, has been marooned indoors, kept there by the conspiring forces of institutional risk aversion, fractured, fearful parenting and the decline of social cohesion. Well-worn admonishments – of the perils of taking your eye off your kids for more than a heartbeat, the obsession with stranger danger, the terror of accidents, the carping about antisocial behaviour – these much-publicised fears are now matched by equally dire warnings from think tanks and psychologists of the toll of 'play deprivation'. As one eminent play theorist, Brian Sutton-Smith, puts it, 'the opposite of play is not work. It's depression.' At the most basic evolutionary level, he argues, our emotional survival is at stake. If excessive caution denies children the time, space and permission to play – *really play*, without some grown-up breathing down their neck – then in the future we will count the social cost in isolated, dysfunctional, angry or even violent adults. The time will come, indeed, when we may wish that we had occasionally judged it better to be sorry than safe.

In 2012, even the Health and Safety folk joined the chorus with a statement in which they maintained, 'When providing play opportunities, the goal is not to eliminate risk, but to weigh up the risks and benefits. No child will learn about risk if they are wrapped in cotton wool.'

Here in Wales, the Assembly government came up with what they called a Play Sufficiency Duty, which despite its somewhat cheerless title pledged to secure opportunities for all children to horse about in the way that children do, or at least they should. In the case of Plas Madoc, a portion of anti-poverty funding was diverted towards play initiatives. And for The Land – which had declined into a grim place where, in the words of one local, 'people got up to bad stuff' – it was to mean a whole new sovereign life.

In October 2011, a fence went up around the plot. The boundary was tagged with jolly graffiti and a team of play workers recruited. Gone was the dog mess, broken glass and the needles, and a miscellany of friendlier garbage was shipped in. Someone fetched hammers and saws from a pound store and two shipping containers were dropped in by crane to be a storeroom and an office for the playground manager. The following February, The Land became Plas Madoc's very own junk playground: not a swing or climbing frame to be seen, nothing fixed, nothing new, nothing in the shape of a cute animal, just heaps of junk that shift, as the days pass, like sand dunes in the Sahara.

Plas Madoc born and bred, Claire Griffiths is the manager of The Land and in large part the architect of its joyful chaos. She sits, swinging slightly as if she would rather be outside playing, on a shabby office chair in the shipping container that is her executive suite. She explains how the place works: how it is not as anarchic as it may look; how vigilant she and her colleagues are whenever The Land opens its gate; how they, in her words, 'loiter with intent', apparently busy with other things, but always with eyes and ears open to what the kids are doing; how well they prepare the site in advance, removing the hazards but retaining the risk; how well the team know the two hundred or so girls and boys registered to come here and play on their own; how few rules there are (the fact that one of them is 'Don't Burn Plastic' may give you some idea); how there are always three play workers present, but how rarely they intervene, leaving the kids to graze their knees, hammer their thumbs, singe their eyebrows, get stuck up trees, have quarrels and make mistakes, largely unmediated by the stodgy common sense of adults.

'When you go to other playgrounds,' Claire says, 'it's all kind of prescriptive, and I knew that that's not what I wanted for The Land. I believed these children could do it themselves and it's not very aesthetically pleasing, but I'm not here to conform to an adult sense of order or tidiness. It's not sanitised, it's wild. And that was the big risk I felt *I* was taking. Are the children going to get this? Are they going to go *but where's the swings, where's the slide?* But they didn't.' She pauses and glances out of the door to the playground beyond. 'They got it. Like, straight away.'

Claire's colleague at Wrexham Council, Mike Barclay, has dropped by and he takes a seat on the other tatty office chair in the shipping container.

If Claire is the architect of The Land, then Mike is arguably the engineer. Ask him about those playgrounds with bucket swings you cannot fall out of, spongy safety surfaces and a seesaw in primary colours and he will shake his head and ask, 'But is that really playing?' Responsible for the encyclopaedia-thick Risk Management Policy for The Land, he points out that when you're doing what he and Claire are doing, you get used to being 'very heavily scrutinised'. To put it politely. And there flows from him a well-rehearsed account of how each and every risk taken at The Land has its own benign doppelgänger in the form of an evidentially sound benefit. He reels off the studies that show how risk teaches children to regulate their emotions, how the shared experience of risk forms strong social bonds, how it develops the wiring of our stress-response systems and attunes the cognitive and behavioural flexibility that will serve these children well in adult life, making them capable and resilient; even, dare one say it, *happy*.

And at the heart of all this sits a remarkably nuanced understanding – one that many a psychologist or political theorist would also recognise – of how very slippery risk can be to define in the first place, yet how seductive and how fundamental to the human relationship with uncertainty.

'I think risk is actually *inherent* in how children play,' Mike says, 'if by risk you mean uncertainty, and play is almost always uncertain because you're never quite sure where it's going to go.'

'The point is,' Claire says, 'that you trust these children, you're not seeing them as incapable or

incompetent. They can come here and they can try and they can fail and they're not judged or assessed or told the right way to do it. They get to figure all that out for themselves. It's important that children can make mistakes and' – Claire shrugs and smiles – 'they survive.'

'And all that uncertainty,' says Mike, '*that* is what makes The Land a good place for playing.'

★ ★ ★

Embracing a particular vein of uncertainty was something of a game at the beginning of the fifteenth century for a small papal bureaucrat with a big name – Poggio Florentinus, Poggio the Florentine.

Canny apostolic secretary by day, Poggio harboured a passion, out of hours, for the fashion-able scholarly hobby of 'book hunting', combing monastic libraries around medieval Europe for long-forgotten manuscripts by Latin writers. He was good at it, unearthing, among others, all twelve volumes of Quintilian's hefty tome on rhetoric, the entirety of Vitruvius's *De Architectura*, several unknown orations by Cicero and various other classical morsels, all of which he had copied and circulated among the learned. But it was on a winter's day early in 1417, in a monastery library no one quite knows where in Germany, that Poggio laid hands on his greatest discovery: a complete copy of a hitherto lost poem by the Epicurean philosopher of the first century BC, Titus Lucretius Carus. It was called *De Rerum Natura,* 'On the Nature of Things', and it contained an idea that would change the world.

Nearly seven and a half thousand lines long and certainly no beach read, *De Rerum Natura* nevertheless bristles with an astounding range of forward-looking ideas. The poem, as rehabilitated by the enterprising Poggio, went on to inspire Shakespeare, Montaigne, Newton, even anticipated Darwin, Einstein, Heisenberg – all of it with an audacious account of a universe not governed by Fate or by the gods, but characterised by the motion of infinitesimal particles, atoms, 'the seeds of things'. Furthermore – and here was Lucretius's killer idea – this atomic world was subject to what he called 'clinamen', a swerve. This swerve was slight and occasional, but unexpected and random in its divergence from predictable and orderly motion. It was, at both atomic level and the human one, what accounted for chance, for the thread of fundamental unpredictability which runs through all our lives. Lucretius's 'swerve' was the very fount of risk.

The poet goes on to counsel a way of living with equanimity within this swerving world, and among the consolations offered is one that is liberating and revelatory to anyone grappling with ideas about risk. Lucretius points out how empowering this essential unpredictability can be, how it 'can annul the decrees of destiny', how it can forestall 'an endless chain of causation'. Indeed, so he argues, this uncertainty is the lifeblood of our free will, of our creativity. And, if we can only teach ourselves to go with the flow, it may just be the foundation of our freedom.

* * *

'Think I can make it?' asks a small boy in a red T-shirt who is standing near the door of Claire Griffiths's office at The Land, squinting up into the sunshine at some older kids who have climbed on top of the shipping container and who are taking it in turns to jump from the top.

'Only you can answer that, mate,' replies a nearby play worker raking a thin layer of detritus across the mud.

'It doesn't hurt,' yells the lad who has just landed on a plastic-swathed mattress.

A lanky boy holding a hammer peers down from the top of the container. Presumably because he does not want to jump holding it, he lobs the hammer off the top. It swivels through the air and hits the ground an inch or two away from the brown

curls of a girl who just has bent down (swerved, you might say) to tie the lace on her trainer. No one bats an eyelid.

The two cousins who began the afternoon by repeatedly jumping onto the old boat come over to talk. The elder of the two says he is called James Greenshields and that he is nine years old.

'I come here a few times a week,' he says, wiping some dirt off his nose with the back of his hand. 'Sometimes I feel like I just want to stay here. I get to build things with wood, hammer nails. Saws, things like that. Sometimes it can be a bit dangerous, like the time I never knew there was a nail pointing up and I jumped down and I got a big hole in my foot.'

'Yeah, and don't forget saws,' adds his cousin helpfully.

'This is Brandon. Yeah, I cut my finger once with the saw, didn't I?'

Brandon nods.

'What I do, jumping off something like that over there, that's my favourite' – James points to a makeshift construction on two levels built around the base of a tree with ply, pallets, two oil drums and an old ladder – 'and it's scary when you're on top, but I just think to myself, "Is that safe? Will I be able to make a perfect landing?" And if I don't, then, well, I don't do it. Like when we was jumping onto the boat earlier, I knew I could do it.' James suddenly changes focus. 'But this summer I want to climb up that tree.' He points. 'That one. Because there's not much branches up there, so it's going to be hard.'

He eyes it in silence for a moment and then 'Here's my dad,' he says, and he races off to squeeze in a swing on the tatty rope over the stream before tea.

Wayne is James's stepfather. He is, he says, raising James and his own son, James's little brother, Taylor, alone, after a long, ugly custody battle with the boys' mother four years ago.

'Because of the way I got custody,' he says, 'I was petrified at first that my boys weren't going to stay with me. So I wouldn't let them play out. I wouldn't even let them play in the garden, to the point where if the door went I'd be shouting *Don't answer it. Don't answer it. Dad'll look through the window.*' Wayne glances over at James, who is hanging upside down impersonating Tarzan on the rope above the brook. 'It's mad to think back that I was like that. I was trying to cover all avenues to keep the boys safe, but the decisions I was making were incredibly unsafe for our long-term plans. So it was a hard one, letting them come here. I didn't know what The Land was or what it represented. And it took me coming down here to understand how we can all become better people by playing a bit more and by learning to take a few more risks in life. The Land is probably the one place where James feels at home. It's a haven really. It's given him freedom.'

Wayne looks down and kicks at a sweet wrapper on the ground. Then he looks up and he says it again.

'Freedom.'

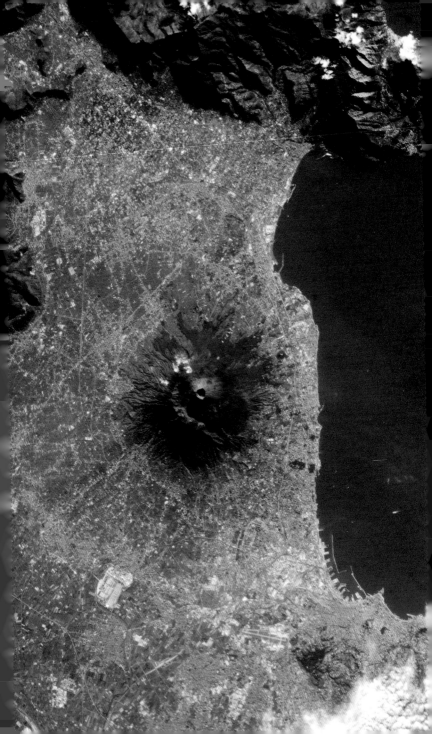

2

Under the volcano

Little did Poggio the Florentine know that the ninth-century copy of *De Rerum Natura* found that frosty day in 1417 was not the only surviving trace of Lucretius's great hymn to our uncertain world.

More than five hundred years after Poggio's death, in the late 1980s, scholars were examining one of nearly two thousand papyrus scrolls excavated from the private library of a wealthy Roman whose fine villa in the seaside resort of Herculaneum had been consigned to oblivion by the eruption of Mount Vesuvius in AD 79. The scrolls themselves, carbonised into lumps, had been preserved beneath thirty metres of volcanic debris. Unearthed in the mid-eighteenth century, they lent their name to what became known as the Villa of the Papyri, but it took a further two centuries and a good deal of modern science besides to unfurl them without reducing the scrolls to dust. Only then could state-of-the-art scanning equipment attempt to identify what these books really were.

The library, it turned out, had housed a large collection of Epicurean philosophy and, lo and behold, among it: fragments of Lucretius's long-lost 'On the Nature of Things'. How strangely fitting that a book calling on humanity to knuckle down and accept the uncertain nature of the world should have so succumbed to the most vivid and violent realisation of risk.

* * *

Giuseppe Mastrolorenzo is, he says, so used to talking about Vesuvius, reading about Vesuvius, thinking and writing about Vesuvius, watching it, climbing it, photographing it, measuring it, smelling and touching it, quarrelling and dreaming about it, that he has neither the energy, nor the head-space, to be actively scared of it. Which is not to say it is not frightening.

'Probably I'm contaminated, if that's the right way of putting it, by the science,' he says. 'Because I've no emotion about it at the moment. I just consider the geological evidence. To witness a catastrophe directly will be different, I know that, but I don't know when in my life, *if* in my life, I'll be there to assist at an eruption of Vesuvius.' He shrugs and looks down at the gravelly tephra by his feet. 'I just don't know,' he says, and looks up with a smile.

A volcanologist with the Osservatorio Vesuviano, the oldest such institute in the world, Giuseppe has spent over thirty years studying the volcano that annihilated Pompeii and Herculaneum and which looms today over modern Naples. Standing on a ledge within the crater formed by the last eruption in 1944, several metres down from its jagged lip and enclosed by walls of rock the colour of pencil lead, Giuseppe seems quite at home.

Fissures in the lichen-silvered crags hiss sulphurous breath at him, like some diabolical steam-bath, while from high above, tiny figures of day-trippers with their cameras and their backpacks peer down into the abyss, silhouetted against the clouds like so many starlings on a rooftop. From what might reasonably pass for the outer shores of Hell, Giuseppe sets about explaining why 'this is the most dangerous volcano in the world'.

On the one hand, it is obvious why. While the old centre of Naples is some fifteen kilometres away, dense suburban sprawl reaches right up the volcano's slopes. Moreover, there is the time-honoured problem of forgetfulness. This is that tendency we all have to weight our intuitive assessment of risk towards what we can most readily recollect, the cognitive bias famously identified by Daniel Kahneman and Amos Tversky in the 1970s as the availability heuristic.

'It's difficult,' says Giuseppe, 'for ordinary people to accept that this is the most dangerous volcano because generation after generation have lived here with no problems. Eruptions are rare compared with the length of a human life, but in geological time, they are very frequent. Entire generations completely forget the risk, but scientists and government, they must remember.'

Giuseppe clearly takes this responsibility of 'remembering' seriously and rather personally. He spends as much as a day a week giving interviews with the express purpose of getting what he knows about Vesuvius out there in the public domain. This afternoon, he says, it is a French TV crew, and

he checks the time of the filming on his mobile phone.

Dr Mastrolorenzo's prolific candour on the severity of the risk posed by the volcano has made him no friends in certain quarters.

'My scientific life has been relatively difficult,' he says. 'I've had problems getting money for research. On the other hand, there's the risk of the scientist who makes an undeclared compromise between risk and benefit as in the case of the L'Aquila earthquake.' He is referring of course to the recent prosecution of seven of Italy's natural disaster experts for manslaughter on the grounds that they gave only what the judge called 'vague, generic and ineffective' warnings before the 6.3 magnitude earthquake that killed 309 people in L'Aquila in 2009.

'That was the first time,' says the volcanologist, wiping away some condensation that has gathered above his eyebrows and examining it, 'that scientists had ever been condemned for being too optimistic. And they went to jail. So this is a risk too.'

But not one that Giuseppe is likely to take any day soon. He launches into a brutally detailed account of what could happen if an eruption were to happen 'tomorrow'. He explains how prone Vesuvius is to explosive eruptions, not those winsome fountains of lava out of volcano central casting, but what is known as a Plinian eruption and is very, very dangerous.

Named after Pliny the Younger's account of his uncle, Pliny the Elder's, demise in the AD 79 eruption, a Plinian eruption (and its smaller cousin, the subplinian) is one in which the top of a volcano effectively explodes, sending a great column of pulverised rock, pumice and hot gas up to thirty-five kilometres into the sky. Pliny wrote in a letter to Tacitus of this cloud being 'like an umbrella pine', the parasol-shaped conifer found in thick groves all over the flanks of Vesuvius, but to modern eyes, the plume following a Plinian eruption looks more like a nuclear explosion. And what happens next, explains Giuseppe, has the potential to be every bit as lethal.

After some hours or even days, this eruptive column begins to collapse, sending forth avalanches of superheated gas and rock that travel at speeds of up to 700 kilometres an hour and can cover large distances, incinerating any sentient creature in their path. It was such pyroclastic flows, as they are called, that did for the townspeople of Pompeii and Herculaneum and would do for the contemporary population in the event of a similar eruption. Having written several papers on an even more catastrophic Bronze Age eruption of Vesuvius that sent pyroclastic matter as far as the present location of downtown Naples and beyond, Giuseppe says that this is the 'worst-case scenario'. A similar eruption today would put a full *three million people* in the firing line.

Yet, despite the monitoring stations around the lip of the crater above Giuseppe with their infrared cameras and gas sensors, this question of when Vesuvius will erupt, and how violently, is simply impossible to answer.

'All these systems can create a false feeling of safety because people say, *Well, they know everything.* No. We know what happened in the past up to one second ago, but we don't know anything about the future. At *this very moment*' – Giuseppe is exercised now, slicing the air with his hand – 'a new crisis could start.'

A black cloud has slid across the sun and there is a rumble of thunder. It is almost as though Giuseppe had stage-managed it to make the point. He talks of the earthquakes over days, weeks or months that would mark the beginning of 'the crisis', the bulges or new outcrops in the rock that would follow, the changes in the gas composition of the crater's steamy emissions and how, below the ground, the vast magma chamber would begin to weaken and fracture.

It is enough to make anyone of a delicate temperament wish to get out of that damned crater without delay, but Giuseppe has not finished. Because his key

point, the point he is here to make, is that the Italian authorities are insufficiently prepared for this and that millions of lives are at stake.

'For many years I have been insisting that the civil defence people change the emergency plan because it is an optimistic emergency plan' – 'optimistic' in this context is clearly a dirty word – 'but the problem, in my experience, is that scientists tend to find some compromise between the requests of government and the evidence. But I completely ignore any requests to have some' – he searches for the word – '*discount*. I can make a discount but nature makes not a discount.' And he lets fly a short hollow laugh.

This 'discount' of Giuseppe's refers to the fact that the current civil defence risk assessment has been drawn up according to the lesser subplinian eruption model, not the full Plinian cataclysm of the Pompeii eruption. On that basis, three zones around the volcano have been designated: the Red Zone, around the cone of Vesuvius and vulnerable to pyroclastic flows, the Yellow Zone, less exposed but susceptible to volcanic fallout, and the Blue, a valley in which there could be landslides. In response to persistent lobbying by Giuseppe and others, the Red Zone was expanded in 2013. It now covers over a quarter of a million people across 24 municipalities, all of whom must be evacuated before an eruption, although quite how remains to be seen. A few years back, the government offered small financial incentives to people to move out of the Red Zone altogether, but so few people took up the offer that the scheme was scrapped. As for those two million or more in the Yellow and Blue zones, they would be required under this plan to watch the erupting volcano and to wait and see whether the prevailing winds made it necessary to leave. It is a proposition at which Giuseppe lets out a yelp of exasperation.

'My personal opinion is that this is absurd,' he says. 'If they want to assume a subplinian eruption they should declare that it's not based on scientific evidence, but because it's too expensive. People say it's impossible to evacuate three million, but it's not. Not in theory.'

You get the sense that this is a quarrel that will run and run, but a key question remains: are the ordinary people who live in the Red Zone crazy to do so at all?

'No, actually I don't think they are,' says

Giuseppe, 'because I think that if you are very accurately informed about the risk, prepared for the evacuation and there is a good system of civil defence that can organise it, then yes, you can live near a volcano, but you must be ready.'

Just before he leaves to meet the French TV crew, Giuseppe Mastrolorenzo lets slip where he himself lives. And all at once, you glimpse the reality of the risk dilemma that has vexed Neapolitans for centuries.

'Where do *I* live? OK, well, I live in the presently considered Yellow Zone that I suggest be changed to Red Zone. And so I guess, according to my own research, I live in the Red Zone too.' Giuseppe grins, shrugs and he is gone.

★ ★ ★

As you drive down from the crater on the old road towards Herculaneum, the souvenir stalls and snack shacks at the summit give way to wooded slopes with far-reaching views over the plain, the sun moving in patches across the city below and the white wakes of boats in the blue bay beyond. By the wayside, old lava flows make turbulent streets through the lush vegetation, and soon there are villas, apartment blocks with balconies for admiring the view, roadside shrines to the Virgin, several pizzerias, a country club. And before long the suburbs crowd in.

It is difficult to judge whether these places speak more of boldness, denial or inertia, but one could do worse than consider an exhortation of the most virile variety from the philosopher Friedrich

Nietzsche, who fell in love with this part of the world in the autumn of 1876.

Around his 32nd birthday and some four years after the previous eruption of Vesuvius, Nietzsche took a long holiday with friends in Sorrento on the Bay of Naples. It was here that the philosopher experienced what can only be described as an intellectual metamorphosis, one that pertains closely to the subject of risk.

Seemingly overnight, Nietzsche turned his back on the glum caution of the philosopher who had most enthralled him as a young man. This was Arthur Schopenhauer, who counselled that the world was 'a kind of hell' and that the only thing to do was to 'procure a small fireproof room' – and, one presumes, sit in it.

But in Sorrento, Nietzsche's thinking changed course. It swerved. Practically overnight, he decided that jeopardy was good, even essential. To embrace it was to embrace all of life, not just the nice, cosy bits. And this, he argued, was what would make you strong, make you live, *truly live* in a way that you could happily repeat over and over, were some Groundhog Day glitch in the universe to send you into a spiral of what Nietzsche calls 'eternal recurrence'.

'For believe me,' he bellowed (from the pages of the book in which he also chanced his arm that God was dead), 'the secret for harvesting from existence the greatest fruitfulness and the greatest enjoyment is – to *live dangerously!* Build your cities on the slopes of Vesuvius! Send your ships into uncharted seas!'

It is heady stuff, but what of its real-world wisdom? We shall come to uncharted seas ere long, but what about those who do, literally, *live dangerously* on the slopes of Vesuvius?

★ ★ ★

Baldassare and Felicia have been married for 63 years.

'Our romance began when she was twelve and I was fourteen. We were in school. Can you imagine?'

Baldassare chuckles and swipes the air with a rough-knuckled hand, his wedding ring held in place by a nugget of Elastoplast wrapped around the thick gold at his palm. Now aged 89 and 87, Baldassare and Felicia have lived all their lives just above a town called Somma Vesuviana, which lies on the northern flank of the volcano, a few kilometres from the vent and just below the lip of an old crater.

Both families, the De Simons (Baldassare's) and the Improtas (Felicia's), have lived on the mountain for many generations, scraping a living from growing fruit, keeping dairy cows and cutting wood. Their forefathers were here at the time of Nietzsche's little holiday and long before, enduring, if one examines the dates, some eight or nine eruptions of the volcano. The couple themselves were in their late teens when Vesuvius last blew in 1944.

'The volcano exploded day after day,' says Baldassare. 'I remember it. Boom. Boom. Boom.' He lets his voice echo around their small, dark

kitchen, with its metal chairs and Formica table, an old wood stove in one corner and a humming fridge in the other, with a small TV set and a Tupperware box of tiny apples on top of it. 'There was lots of smoke and from inside that smoke, it spewed out boiling rain that ruined soil and crops. Our fruit trees were "cooked", vines as well. And then the eruption itself came.'

'I remember rocks and soil raining down,' says Felicia. 'We put barrels on our heads for protection. And do you know what was really scary? I remember when the lava was coming down from Vesuvius, me and my friend went to see it. We got close. It was only a hundred metres from us. I remember apricot trees falling and bursting into flames.'

'But thankfully,' adds her husband, 'Somma was not hit by the eruption itself, although three huge rocks came out of the crater, as big as this house. One fell in our field and the other two nearby.' Baldassare sighs and shakes his head. 'Yes, that volcano never did us any good.'

'I was the oldest of eight,' says Felicia, 'so there were children running everywhere. Our parents could do nothing but trust in divine providence.' She bows her head for a second towards a calendar that is tacked to the wall and pictures the Virgin Mary with a crowned infant Jesus in her lap. A silver rosary is draped over one corner.

A brief silence follows, then Baldassare says, briskly, 'But we never thought of leaving Somma. We had a house, some land, and the truth is we liked it here. There was a sense of anxiety for a while after the eruption, but that dwindled as time passed. They've even built restaurants under the volcano now.' And he opens his eyes wide.

'We're here now,' says Felicia. 'If the mountain erupts, there is very little we can do. It is destiny.'

'And in my opinion, that's not living with a risk,' says Baldassare. 'I was born here. I grew up here. I will die here. I've never been afraid up here. We have animals, land, fresh and clean air.' Baldassare pauses, searching for the right words. 'We hunt hares.'

'We have all we need,' says Felicia, quietly. 'Thank God.' And she gets up to wipe the table.

Just then their neighbours and friends, the Sessa family, drop by, mother Assunta, father Giovanni and their 28-year-old son, Giuseppe. Someone brings out a tinfoil platter laden with fruit from the orchard outside and thimble-sized glasses are filled with brandy for a toast: 'In the face of those who wish us ill, *salute*!'

Both Assunta and Giovanni's families have also lived in Somma for generations. Although

they were born after the '44 eruption, each grew up with stories of their parents running across the fields with cooking pots on their heads to protect against the steaming hail of rocks and of how a few unlucky houses collapsed under the weight of the fallout. Yet, perhaps without first-hand experience of the mountain's ancient wrath, more modern hazards have drifted to the fore. We all live on Vesuvius; that is what they seem to be saying.

'There are plenty of other risks in the rest of life,' is how Assunta puts it, clearing the tiny glasses onto a tray, 'riskier than living on the sides of Vesuvius. We can't control what happens inside the mountain; it's Nature and there's nothing we can do about it. It's human actions I fear, risks generated by people, crime. We used to not even lock the front door at night. Now we live in jails, with iron bars on windows and alarm systems.'

Assunta moves to follow the others outside into the orchard. 'I've come to realise,' she says, crossing the concrete veranda where a small dog is fast

asleep, 'these fears are different: fear of an eruption and fear in daily life. The volcano is a collective fear. My daughter says she hopes if the volcano wakes up, that we are all together, that we can face whatever comes together. But those ordinary daily risks are yours alone. They're not shared.'

Outside the air is clear. Boughs heavy with apricots, grapes, lemons and plums are tinged pink by the setting sun. There's a mockingbird in a ply and chicken-wire enclosure that rants in Neapolitan dialect when anyone walks by. And through palms, the lip of the volcano above looks soft and mossy and green. Now that no one is talking about Vesuvius, the mood has lifted and the two families are chatting, laughing. Giovanni smokes a cigarette. They all look out at the view and Giuseppe says, 'You see. It's beautiful, isn't it?'

And it is hard to say whether this is what *living dangerously* should look like or means, but in the warm glow of sunset and of family, it looks good.

3

The price of happiness

Hanging across a threshold at the back of Tetsuro Hama's restaurant in a London Soho backstreet is an iconic and rather optimistic image of a volcano. Reproduced from one of Hokusai's famous *Thirty-Six Views of Mount Fuji*, the picture is called 'Fine Wind, Clear Morning', and in it, the crimson peak runs with melted snow. It has been printed onto a *noren*, the gashed panel of fabric traditionally used to divide kitchen from dining room in Japanese homes, or in a commercial setting to indicate that you are open for business. Waiters emerge, as if by magic, through Fuji's lower slopes bearing long, canoe-like plates of sushi and sashimi, lacquered boxes filled with tempura that look like the little clouds in Hokusai's picture, earthenware bowls of steaming noodles and wooden boards of Wagyu beef that have been cooked on the restaurant's own 'yogan-yaki', a natural lava grill made of volcanic rock imported from Mount Fuji itself.

As one waits for one's lunch with rumbling tum, it passes the time to ponder the difference between the sort of risk embodied by a volcano and that inherent in the modest business venture that turns a profit, or hopes to, by selling people nice things to eat.

The distinction between the two is not so very different from that described by Assunta in Somma Vesuviana as she spoke of the anxiety slippage within her generation from worrying about Vesuvius to worrying about other people instead. Indeed, this power shift in our relationship with risk, this augmented sense of human agency and of risks, small and large, thrumming away on all sides, is a key marker of modern life – or 'modernity', as you call it if you are a sociologist, like Ulrich Beck, for instance, or Anthony Giddens, both revered expositors of the famous contention that we are now living in a 'Risk Society'.

Among Beck and Giddens's arguments is the idea that external risks (volcanoes, epidemics and the like) have been superseded by 'manufactured' ones, risks of our own making. Be it from the melting icecaps, from superbugs born of antibiotic misuse, or for that matter from home-grown jihadis who blow themselves up on commuter trains, this manufactured risk is now so ubiquitous in contemporary life that we calibrate near-as-damn-it everything else in relation to it. It is not, they reason, that there is *more* risk today than there was in days of old; rather that the position it occupies in our lives has changed beyond recognition.

But there is an upside to our often neurotic obsession with what is going to happen in the future. Because as well as worrying about what can go wrong, we also devote considerable personal energy to imagining what can go right. We hope. We dream. Less beholden than ever before to divine providence or to tradition, we have cultivated the

belief that we are the authors of our own lives, facing an uncertain world that is undeniably full of hazards, but also full of delicious possibility.

And delicious sushi. For lunch has arrived and, with it, the entrepreneur behind this Soho restaurant, Tetsuro Hama. His is not a story of fire and flood, or of high-rolling poker-game financial jeopardy. No Jordan Belfort antics here. Instead it is a story of quiet risk that is as personal as it is pecuniary, a modest tale about having the nerve to follow your heart and to be just a little bit entrepreneurial about your own happiness.

Over a plate of jewel-like pillows of rice and fish, Tetsuro tells how he was born in Okaya in central Japan just after the war and how his father was a businessman, although not a particularly lucky one. Hama Senior had run an import-export business on the Chinese mainland before Tetsuro was born, but when Japan lost the war, the business collapsed, and soon after his first wife died of TB.

'He lost everything,' says Tetsuro, nudging a

stray grain of rice with a slim black chopstick. 'He just had a new baby, my brother, and whatever baggage he could carry in his hands, that's all he had left.'

Undeterred, Tetsuro's father made for the capital, 'the almost totally burnt-out Tokyo town', where he opened a small coffee shop and a hundred-yen store, the Japanese equivalent of a dime store or pound shop. But, to the chagrin of the wider Hama family, both ventures flopped.

'My father has always been a role model to me,' says Tetsuro, 'because he was a very flexible person, very open to ideas. He tried many, many things. That, I think, I learned from him. But his brothers and other relatives were always saying *oh, he's not concentrating on one thing, he's not successful.* And I, as a child, felt that's not right, it's not very fair.'

This sense of injustice and belief that one should be permitted to run the risk of failure by trying something new – and to do so without reproach – was, for Tetsuro, a feeling that refused to go away. Indeed, it was to become his lifelong credo.

In 1971, at the age of 23, he left Japan for the first time, part of the first wave of post-war tourism as long-standing travel restrictions were relaxed. While most headed for America, Tetsuro was one of a handful that made for Europe.

'I wanted to be different from the crowd,' he says, calmly rotating a bowl of miso soup on the table as if it were a dial. 'I don't generally go with the majority and when I got here I felt it was just a new world, everything so different to what I'd been brought up with. And I wanted to stay.'

Tetsuro had long nursed an aspiration to follow his father into business and it was an idea that clicked as soon as he realised he could do so away from the censorious gaze of his extended family. He returned to Tokyo, but instead of settling down to a humdrum job as was expected, he declared to his parents, 'I want to start up a business. *Abroad.*'

'I did not want to do something ordinary,' he says. 'And most parents at that time would have said *no way, you can't*. But my father?' He smiles. 'He said, *Ah, that's a good idea; you do it*. It was reckless of me to think that I could do this with no money, no language, no contacts, but I had nothing to lose and it was an adventure.'

There is a slight incongruity in hearing these unruly words tumble from this slight, neat man in carefully pressed clothes of beige and mid-blue, his hair greying at the temples, an orderly moustache. Indeed, there is little outward sign of Tetsuro Hama's resistance to conformity, but for a twinkle of exuberance that dances in his eyes and an informality of manner that does not quite match his outward demeanour.

In 1973 he arrived in London and started looking for opportunities at once. Before long, he stumbled upon a small tourist hotel in a Bayswater backstreet that had a breakfast room in the basement unused for the rest of the day. With only four or five Japanese restaurants in London at that time, and now ever-increasing numbers of tourists from Japan, Tetsuro set about persuading the hotel proprietor that droves of Japanese clientele would beat a path to his door if only there were a Japanese restaurant on the premises.

'I said, *Well, if I just rented it out for nothing,* and he said, *Nothing? Oh no, no, no. You have to pay the electricity and the gas, OK?* And I agreed.' He giggles, apparently as tickled by this today as he was forty years ago.

Tetsuro set about making his own restaurant in a manner that sounds more like a school project than a bold entrepreneurial foray. He cut out a map of Japan from a sheet of polystyrene, painted it and stuck it to the wall. Then with wood and wallpaper he knocked up a shoji screen to cover the window that overlooked the basement steps. And he opened for business.

'I called it Japanese Grill Room Hama. "Grill Room" because, a very simple reason, raw fish was not readily available and my chef, he's not a sushi chef. He's a French chef, Japanese, but a very young boy, he's only nineteen, just graduated from cooking academy, so I say to this guy, *OK, can you make a miso soup? Oh yeah,* he says, *I can do miso soup.* And I say, *Right, that's it, you come.* And so he came.'

Tetsuro roars with laughter. In the course of lunch, he relives what seem to be his happiest memories in this playscript idiom. But behind the repartee, you can see that the older man is keenly aware of what was as stake.

'So it's all a huge risk, isn't it?' he says, composing himself and adjusting the angle of his chopstick rest. 'I knew nothing about running a restaurant.

I knew nothing about business and I didn't even have a work permit. You know, worst-case scenario, deported perhaps.' He raises his eyebrows. 'But it's just one of the elements of my character. By nature I'm very optimistic, so in that way I'm a risk-taker, but don't feel it as risk. Also sometimes if you *don't* take the risk, that is a risk itself.'

Japanese Grill Room Hama was no overnight success, but within a year they broke even and Tetsuro even began to pay himself a small salary. A second restaurant opened three years later on the Finchley Road. And it was in 1979 that he spotted the opportunity which would make his fortune.

At the same time as travel restrictions had lifted in Japan at the beginning of the seventies, so too did the red tape on individual buyers importing cars. Such was Tetsuro's networking ability, not to mention his relative ease with the British business environment and grasp of the language, that Japanese car enthusiasts began asking him to source a Ferrari here or a Jaguar there on their behalf. It was exciting.

'If it's routine, I just can't do it,' he says, leading the way out of the restaurant with a wave over his shoulder and the brisk step of a man half his age to the silver Mercedes parked outside. 'I always have to find something new,' he says, starting the engine. And as the warm summer wind seems to waft Mr Hama's Mercedes up Portland Place and across Regent's Park, past the mansion blocks of Maida Vale, the mid-rise concrete of Swiss Cottage and round the less than tranquil North Circular, towards his other shop floor, he describes how this impromptu move into buying and selling cars evolved.

He started out renting a tiny office at the back of a large garage and showroom, subcontracting their engineering services, selling on their cars, all with the express purpose of becoming the go-to supplier within the Japanese community for all things motoring. It was a smart idea and the business expanded rapidly. By the mid-1990s, Tetsuro found himself at the helm of the largest Toyota dealership in the country, turning over around £70 million a year. But at the same time it became 'not boring exactly but routine', he says, and stressful too, 'pressure growing and growing'. All money and no fun was not the Hama way. In 2003, he spotted an exit and sold the business for what he calls 'quite a reasonable amount of money'. Now standing in the middle of surely the cleanest garage you will ever see and the only part of the car business Tetsuro retained, he says simply, 'This was a chance to get out and do something else.'

After some months, a call came in from Kaoru Yamamoto, his original nineteen-year-old chef from the first restaurant and still a friend, who was miserably running a failing French bistro in recession-hit Tokyo.

'So he said, *I just want to close it*, and I said, *And what's the plan?*' – Tetsuro is smiling again from ear to ear – '*Nothing*, he says. *Nothing? Would you like to come back to London?* Because Japanese food is booming now. And he came. I just do it for him,' Tetsuro lowers his voice to a whisper, 'for the sake of Mr Yamamoto, for my chef. He's very talented.'

And so it was that he and Kaoru Yamamoto came full circle and began the elegant restaurant in Soho with the volcano *noren* over the kitchen door. A Japanese cookery school in the City followed, opening its doors to coincide with the 2013 announcement that Japanese food culture had been inscribed on the UNESCO register of Intangible Cultural Heritage of Humanity.

'And I might do a chain of fast food,' says Tetsuro, and grins.

Tetsuro Hama is now 66 and, despite spending more than two-thirds of his life in Britain, remains stolidly Japanese. He speaks English with a strong, occasionally impenetrable accent and clearly retains an identity that makes landfall out beyond the Sea of Japan. His wife and grown-up children all returned to Tokyo, but for better or worse, Tetsuro has stayed. The entrepreneurial life he has

enjoyed as a result could not have been undertaken anywhere else, built as it is around a deep understanding of what it is to be a foreigner abroad and how sometimes it is the little things that can make you feel happy and at home.

Asked whether he believes he has had more freedom to pursue his career here in the UK than he would have in his homeland, he says, 'Yeah. I think so,' and he mulls it over, as he walks back towards his car. 'Often in Japan you guarantee the business with your own assets, so if you fail you lose everything. Also Japanese people tend to feel that once you fail, you're a failure, your life is finished. Here you can try again, that's the difference.'

This sits at the heart of Tetsuro's modus operandi and his success. It is one that has long relied upon shrugging off the small failures, of keeping his eyes and his mind open to such thistledown as the zephyrs of good fortune waft his way and then, in his words, 'grabbing it' as it floats past. He is a fine exemplar of that time-honoured combination of being lucky, but also of making your own luck in a Risk Society and an uncertain world.

Another drive across the capital and towards suppertime, Tetsuro breezes into his cookery school, down a side street among the crystalline business temples of Aldgate. He stands around joking with the staff, who are preparing for the evening's class, arranging steel bowls and little dishes of spring onions and wasabi, shiny aubergines and sharp knives. There is the tang of soy and rice vinegar in the air. Someone dares Tetsuro to put on an apron. 'Now that is something I'd like to see,' says one of the chefs, and Tetsuro mimes mock horror. Everyone laughs.

'If I accomplish something I want to achieve then that's my joy,' he says, 'not necessarily a high turnover, not necessarily money. My staff enjoy themselves, it's like a family, very friendly, and that's an achievement. I'm very pleased to see them happy, because then, well, I feel happy as well.'

As the American novelist Jonathan Safran Foer wrote, 'You cannot protect yourself from sadness without protecting yourself from happiness.' And, so Tetsuro Hama's life seems to quietly prove, where would be the joy in that?

4

Étoile

Imagine a very hot surface, a stage of such scalding temperature that you or I would surely be unable to walk across it for fear of burning our feet. And now imagine that a lovely, diaphanous creature comes whirling out of the surrounding blackness and, to a frenetically joyful melody played by unseen musicians, dances there on the tips of exquisite toes. If she were to linger too long, or make one slow, lumpish move, she would surely catch fire. Or so it seems. For instead, smiling as if there is nowhere she would rather be, she spirals and sways and flutters like a white down-feather caught in an eddy of hot wind. Anon, she spins to a triumphant stop and a great cheer of admiration, of disbelief, goes up from the audience.

The stage is not heated, of course. Nor is the figure upon it any kind of supernatural entity. That is just the effect that Ms Dorothée Gilbert is capable of conjuring on a good day at the office. For she is among the finest ballerinas of her generation, an 'étoile' with the Paris Opéra Ballet and based at the confection of gold and statuary that is the Palais Garnier in the centre of the French capital. 'Étoile' is the highest rank of soloist here (literally, a 'star')

and this is the oldest and one of the foremost ballet companies in the world.

Yet Dorothée's eponymously stellar position owes much to a small-scale and not particularly glamorous risk undertaken quietly by her parents nearly twenty years ago. It was the kind of optimistic gamble with which Tetsuro Hama might identify, underpinned as it was by an intuition that happiness is probably worth pursuing, even if one cannot be entirely sure of pinning it down.

For so it was that in the summer of 1995, Richard and Eve Gilbert decided to sell their family business in Toulouse, a modest but long-running concern that manufactured blouses. The couple's only child, eleven-year-old Dorothée – who loved to dance, *lived* to dance – had just been offered a place at the celebrated Paris Opéra Ballet School. Both parents had been to boarding school themselves and hated it, so there would be none of that for Dorothée. If she was going to the capital, then so were they. It was impulsive to say the least. The Gilberts knew nothing of the dog-eat-dog world of ballet, nor how likely it was that if little Dorothée failed to deliver on her promise, and deliver quickly, she would be turfed out within months. Two-thirds of her nine-strong class were gone within the first year. Nor indeed did M. et Mme Gilbert know exactly what is was that they were going to do in Paris to keep the family afloat. A vague hope that they might buy and run one of those iconic Parisian press kiosks was dashed by the realisation that these places changed hands for exorbitant prices. Still, they were here now and Dorothée at the ballet school, so her father simply picked up the phone and piece by piece set about recreating the company he had run in Toulouse.

'So he started from scratch when he was nearly fifty years old,' says Dorothée, who is stirring sweeteners into an expensive *café au lait* in a 9th Arrondissement bar, a stone's throw from the Opéra Garnier. 'And that was a huge risk. *Huge*. I think it must have been psychologically very hard for them to say at that stage, *Right, let's start all*

over again. But they never made me feel that this
was some big thing they were doing for me. They
never said, *Do you realise we came to Paris for you?*
Never. And I think it was fundamental for me that
they were here. Because living at boarding school
with the other little dancers, it's not quite that they
put broken glass in your ballet shoes, but there's a
lot of competition and the atmosphere is difficult.
And, you see, I could escape. I'd go home to my
mum and dad and we'd talk about other things. I
think that was very important for my psychological
balance.'

In Dorothée's line of work, psychological
balance is of material importance. Because,
although clearly not actually dangerous per se, this
is one of those vocations in which a veritable crowd
of risks jostle. On any given day, ballet dancers lay
themselves open to physical injury, professional
failure or personal ridicule, each of these perils
triple-distilled by virtue of the fact that they are
played out in front of an audience.

Her face bright and open, Dorothée wastes no
time in enumerating these manifold jeopardies
over coffee. She speaks in her strong Toulouse
accent of how as an 'étoile' you carry the reputational responsibility of constant excellence, 'always
the creative risk', as she puts it, 'of *is my performance
going to please? Will it work? Will it move the audience?*
Because I must live up to the title I've been given.'
This is a feeling compounded, she says, even today,
by the sense that the legendary Garnier stage is 'a
sacred place', where you must be nothing less than
magnificent, even if the gilded auditorium is empty.

Dorothée is warming to her theme now. There is also, she says, 'the technical risk' – will your feet be able to handle the choreography; and by way of example, she throws off a little story of how the fiendish footwork of the solo that opened this chapter had once caused her to fall flat mid-performance in Cuba. There is a personal risk too, she continues, still smiling beatifically, 'because in the embodiment of characters, you bare all, you reveal your inner self. And so, if the interpretation isn't popular, your own personality is on the line.'

And finally, as if all that were not enough to put anyone in their right mind off ever donning a pink satin slipper again, there is what the delicate art of ballet can do to your body.

'The greatest risk for me,' says Dorothée, leaning forward and absent-mindedly coiling a hand around the back of one ankle, 'is the risk of injury. Because you're always pushing the limits, you get lots of cramps and inflammations that aren't too serious. Those are a dancer's everyday scratches.' She gives a little shrug. 'But the limit that will turn the scratch into a real injury is so fine that it's very difficult to tell where it is. Often, you can hurt yourself without being able to see it coming.'

She disappears, highly animated and with scarcely a frown, into a blood-curdling litany of her injuries, including an account of how, halfway through a performance of *La Bayadère* in 2012, her calf muscle simply ripped spontaneously in two.

'Snap!' she says, her eyes wide. 'I was fine before the show, I'd warmed up and there I was, dancing, ta tatataaaah' – she makes arabesque arms in the air for a moment – 'and then, all of a sudden, all the magic, the suspension, the stress, everything … Snap! As if I woke up from a nightmare. Click! It was horrible. I left the stage like this.' Dorothée gets up from the table and with her hands on her hips shuffles slowly across the empty bar, her head bowed. 'The music kept going, the dancers carried on dancing behind me and I left, just like this. All that existed was my calf and me and the wings to go to.' She returns to the table and, saying 'Do you mind?', she takes out an e-cigarette and inhales on it.

The calf itself healed quickly, just a month to mend and another for physiotherapy, but the psychological healing turned out to be a slower, more complex process. It seems that the injured dancer's relationship with risk needs as much rehabilitation as the torn muscles. For indeed, Dorothée goes so far as to say that the careers of dancers terminated by injury are really always terminated instead by the *psychological toll* of injury, worn out as the dancers are by long-term pain, fearful of more and simply no longer loving what they do, 'not wanting it any more', as she puts it.

'This calf of mine was horrible psychologically, terrible, it shocked me,' she says, with the most sombre face she is to wear all morning. Then she looks down and smoothes a painted fingernail with the pad of her thumb. 'It's difficult not to be scared of getting hurt again. That's a fear that's so strong it stayed with me for a long time, you know, a voice in my head, saying *be careful, don't let everything go, don't give it everything you've got.'* She sighs and then smiles again. 'You really need to build up that confidence in your body again, to know that it won't let you down during the show. The only thing that can do that is time and dancing again, going on stage, doing more shows. And in the end, you realise that you're all right.'

Then Dorothée rises like elegant smoke from her chair – 'Come, I have a class at eleven' – and she sets off up the rue de la Paix towards the Opéra with that distinctive ballet dancer's gait, brisk, just a fraction high-stepped and with the toes of her sequined pumps turned out.

★ ★ ★

The etymology of the word 'risk' turns out to be almost as nomadic as the concept itself. It

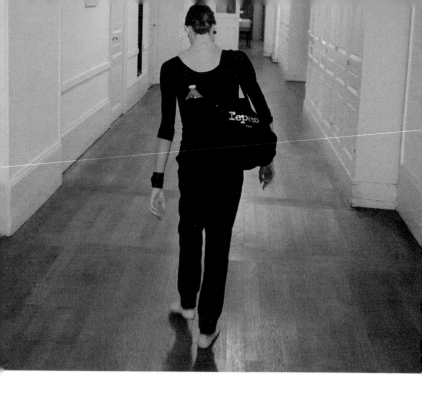

is believed to be traceable back to a story from Homer's *Odyssey*, in which our hero is the sole survivor of a terrible storm sent by Zeus in a fit of celestial pique. Swept back by the sea to the horrid whirlpool-maw of Charybdis, Odysseus's vessel is sucked from beneath him and he is delivered only by clinging onto the roots of a fig tree that happen to be sticking out of the cliff above. The term for one of these roots was 'rhizikon', and from here the word began its own lexical wanderings. Soon also used to mean cliff or 'the cut of firm land', 'rhizikon' cropped up as ancient Greek navigational shorthand for the kinds of 'difficulty' one would do well to avoid at sea. Which may seem a bit mild for Charybdis, but there you have it.

Onwards into Latin the word meandered, where it now appeared as 'resicum', meaning 'that which cuts, rock, crag'. This inference of some kind of edge or jumping-off point beyond which who knows what peril might lie seems then to have finally coalesced in medieval Italian with the word 'risicare', to run into danger, 'risco'.

So it was that, as the great age of maritime exploration got under way in the late Middle Ages, 'risk' now came of age both as a word and as an idea. All over Europe, enterprising merchants and mariners were forsaking the known for the unknown, 'the cut of firm land' for the promise of knowledge and riches across the uncharted sea. This meant running into danger, for sure, but also the possibility of reward. And with this new positive spin, the word was now feverishly borrowed from the Italian, dominoing to the French 'risque', the German 'risiko', the Portuguese 'risco', the Spanish 'riesgo' and, by the 1660s, to the English 'risk'.

You will recall how the philosopher Friedrich Nietzsche, carried away by the holiday mood, exhorted us 'to *live dangerously*', urging not only that we set about building cities on Mount Vesuvius, but also that we should sail our ships 'into uncharted seas'. That is, as we now know, quite literally the definition of risk. Yet in the real world, risk exists not only at sea but all over the place; nor is it, as Dorothée Gilbert's taxonomy of the risks in ballet shows, confined to objective (and calculable) physical jeopardy. Anyone serious about understanding the human face of risk must acknowledge that often intense subjectivity comes into play. So – and here is the problem – how to measure it?

A recent attempt came in the form of a psychometric scale published in 2002 by a team of North American psychologists in which they sought to assess our relationship with risk-taking across five different 'domains' or areas of our decision-making lives. Nattily titled DOSPERT (Domain Specific Risk Taking) and now a pillar of decision theory, the scale categorised the risks people take into those that are ethical (say, forging a signature or having an affair with someone's else wife), financial (investing a slice of your income in speculative stock, or punting a day's wages on the horses), health-related (sunbathing without your factor 30 or perhaps walking home alone at night through a dodgy area), recreational (skiing or skydiving) and social (vocal disagreement with an old friend or changing career in middle age).

On the one hand, responses to a DOSPERT survey built around these different strands of risk reinforced what we already knew intuitively: that people vary a great deal in the risks they are prepared to take but that not one of us is entirely risk averse, or comprehensively risk-taking. Think of the shy base-jumper, or the prudent investor who smokes like a chimney. What was to prove revelatory, however, was the way in which DOSPERT measured for the first time how these variations emanate less from some deep-seated personality trait or fundamental personal attitude to risk and more from how we perceive and weigh the pros and the cons of each specific activity.

Put like that, you suddenly realise just how bespoke our relationship with risk is; how it is not simply about our fear thresholds or even necessarily our appetite for adventure (or ocean travel), but about what we believe in. It is about what we value, what we want our lives to be.

★ ★ ★

Dorothée Gilbert now sits in her dressing room at the Opéra Garnier. It lies backstage off a broad corridor the colour of *café crème*, an immaculate little space with a worn wooden floor, high ceiling and a linen drape at the tall window. Tutus hang on a row of hooks and there are shelves of ballet magazines and folded jumpers. At the end of a couch of plum-coloured velvet are stacked more than a hundred pairs of pointe shoes. 'Two years' supply,' says Dorothée. On the dressing table propped beneath the illuminated mirror is a photograph of a young Rudolf Nureyev, who led the company through the 1980s and whose funeral took place in the marble foyer downstairs.

'There is always a little bit of stage fright before a show and my stomach is in knots' – says Dorothée, pinning up her hair – 'but once I've gone past the curtain, out of the wings, and I'm on stage, I forget everything. And then it can be beautiful, like you're suspended between two worlds. Like you're no longer in the present, no longer earthbound, time has stopped. Just like that.' She snaps her fingers. 'And that's what I love about dancing. It's not like that at every performance. But when it does happen, it's magical.'

There is little doubt what Dorothée values, what she believes in, what makes all the work, all the hardship, all the risk worth it. She is in her way a neat demonstration of the principles of DOSPERT, and not least because her value system and her understanding of risk are at this very moment in the process of being overhauled. For she has only just returned to work after the birth of her first baby, a little girl called Lily, three months ago. Not that you would guess it from her sylph-like frame, but this eleven months off dancing carried its own sense of 'well, not quite risk, but an underlying anxiety', Dorothée says, 'of *will I manage to get my physique back? Manage to dance like before? Will I in the meantime be forgotten?* Because we dancers

control our bodies, our muscles. And all of sudden, I wasn't in control of anything. For the first time, my body changed without it being the result of willpower. It was just natural. So I saw myself with a huge stomach and wondered, *Is it possible to get back to what I was before?* But I have always relied on hard work and saw that it could happen with work again.'

She explains that her debut show back at the Opéra Garnier is to be the notoriously technically difficult *Études* by Lander, 'so I'll be stressed out about that', she says, and she laughs, 'but becoming a parent puts a lot of things into perspective, things I might have blown out of proportion before. Because you have this other little person that's far more important than anything, so the stress or the risk is transferred, in a way.'

* * *

Downstairs, tucked upstage of the auditorium, behind great steel banks of lights and heavy back-stage drapes, is one of the Opéra Garnier's hidden gems. This is the Foyer de la Danse, written of by Balzac, painted by Degas, and a room of such burnished opulence that it is hard to believe it is used only by the company dancers to warm up before the show or to receive notes from the *maître de ballet*.

There, beneath two colossal chandeliers that bloom from the golden plasterwork like small trees, Dorothée warms up for her class. She looks tiny next to the coiled pillars of polished gilt and vast paintings of Arcadian scenes. Indeed, if there were ever a space to reinforce the weight of artistic expectation, the burden of creative risk, upon her slender shoulders, then this is surely it. And so it with some relief that one recollects something remarkably wise that Dorothée said earlier over breakfast coffee in the bar:

'You ask me for a lesson learned?' she said. 'Well, it's good to take risks because that's what makes us surpass ourselves. But at the same time, you need to be aware of what binds you to reality and not go too far and slip into negative risk. You know, like those helium balloons that go up and up? If there wasn't that piece of string tying them to the ground, they'd go off into the sky and you'd never see them again. It's a bit like that. You need the beauty of the balloon but you also need that piece of string. You need to be conscious of what you're doing and of who you are, so that you don't go too far.'

5

The skyline

Mention black swans in some quarters and people will hear Tchaikovsky and think of Odette's nemesis in *Swan Lake*, or perhaps of Natalie Portman cracking up in that photogenic way of hers in her Oscar-winning ballet thriller. But in other circles, dancing will be the last thing that springs to mind. There, heads will fill instead with images of planes hitting the Twin Towers, waves slamming into Fukushima, the on-screen flicker of tumbling stock markets. This association is all thanks to the influential work of the Lebanese-American contrarian and statistician Nassim Nicholas Taleb. His Black Swan theory examines the extreme impact of a certain class of unpredictable and unprecedented event and how the human mind comes to terms with such events by cooking up a retrospective explicability for them, a kind of shaggy-dog story of how we really should have seen them coming all along. We are, argues Taleb, blind to randomness, given to critically underrating the relevance of what we do not know and delusional as to our own powers of prediction. Indeed, we are not, if Taleb is to be believed, half so risk wise as we think we are.

The archetypal Black Swan for this generation

is, of course, 9/11. Taleb, like so many contemporary writers on risk, makes a beeline for it and it would seem rude not to momentarily join them. For 9/11 has become an echo chamber for the full gamut of current thinking about fear, uncertainty, morality, mortality, power and knowledge in the form of that peach of Rumsfeldian rhetoric: the trinity of 'known knowns', 'known unknowns' and 'unknown unknowns'. It has become a kind of phantasm of our darkest feelings about risk.

* * *

But meeting Timothy D. Lynch encourages one to think again. For 9/11 happened on his shop floor and, besides, randomness is something he goes out of his way to tame. Head of the forensic engineering unit at the City of New York Buildings Department, Tim has little time for what he calls 'some huge philosophical discussion' about what makes buildings go up or come down. He is, he says, more of a 'this is what we're gonna do and this is how we're gonna do it' kind of guy, his lack of sentiment tempered by a powerful urge to make things right. For thirteen weeks straight after the 9/11 attacks, Tim volunteered nights, on top of his day job, helping to clear the eighteen-acre debris field around the World Trade Center.

'And it wasn't for everybody,' he says. 'I never found it dangerous but it was a dirty site.'

Asked whether by that he means distressing, Tim says, 'No.'

'Because there's nothing you can do about somebody that's already gone on their road. That's

why I'm OK with this type of work.' He smoothes a crease on one of his sleeves. 'And I've seen plenty. You know, construction accidents, fires. I just put it in a different place. It doesn't mean you can't be humane, but it doesn't keep me awake.' He glances out of the window for a moment across lower Manhattan to where the new World Trade Freedom Tower has recently topped out. 'No, the people I'm really interested in are the ones that are warm and have a pulse.' And he smiles.

It is this often ferocious pragmatism about what he can and what he cannot control, combined with a near-superhuman appetite for work, which has won Tim Lynch a unique position in New York City life. It is also what sits at the heart of his particular form of risk wisdom.

First responders at any disaster to strike at the built environment here (like the 2014 Harlem gas explosion or Hurricane Sandy in 2012), Tim and his

35-strong team are also responsible for the day-to-day health of the city's architecture. That means ensuring that no building in the Five Boroughs presents a serious risk to the people (warm and with a pulse) inside it or down on the streets below. 'I have every building in New York City' is how Tim puts it, and he is not being grandiose. He launches, with the rapid-fire delivery of a racing commentator, into an account of his portfolio.

'OK. Even though there are a million buildings you can parcel them up instantly. So what do I have? I have wood-framed single-family homes, I have garages. I have row houses, nineteenth-century, they're everywhere and I've got 300,000 of those things here in my head instantly.' He taps his forehead. 'All low tenements, 120,000 six-storey buildings, they're mine too. So now I've got a half a million buildings in my head. Then I've got 15,000 houses of worship and we have crucifixes coming off the top, we've got spires falling over, we had bits of stones falling down at St John the Divine the other day. Landmark buildings? That's in my portfolio, 40,000 of them. Tall buildings, apartments and high rises over seven storeys? They're all in my portfolio, 13,500 of those. And construction accidents, crane failures, fatality, fire and all of that stuff.' He glances at his BlackBerry, tapping it silently, as if there is something he must not forget. Then he leaps to his feet and says, 'Now c'mon, I'll show you the shop.'

To describe Tim Lynch as a dynamo would be something of an understatement. A slight but sinewy man of five foot eight, every aspect of him, body and mind, seems taut, primed to move at lightning speed, without ever quite seeming hurried. It is a Saturday morning on a holiday weekend, but he has been at the office since 7 a.m. His uniform is pressed, his shoes shiny. He says things like, 'What makes this city run? Coffee! I run on coffee.' And you can believe it. He clearly does not like to sit still for any length of time. Stepping briskly across the polished floor of the Buildings Department boardroom, he sets off at a lick down a dark corridor toward the forensic engineering unit.

Asked as he walks, 'How do you relax, Tim?', he replies, 'I run.'

Pushing through a double swing door with both hands, Tim arrives with a little gust of moving air, in a large, low-ceilinged office. It is crammed with desks piled high with paperwork and separated from one other by upholstered screens the colour of cooling porridge. On every spare surface, every ledge, every shelf, even in stacks on the floor, there is pile upon pile of paperwork.

'So this is the engine room,' he says. 'I wish it looked better but that's just the way it is. We do a lot of work in here. And it's all about managing risk. A hundred per cent of it.'

He explains how this most iconic of urban landscapes is also uniquely friable, thanks to the extremes of weather, the built-in obsolescence of the otherwise ambitious architecture and the predominantly rental culture that means often remote owners do not take as much care of their ailing buildings as they would if they lived in them.

With a polished toe, Tim points out a large

block of masonry under a desk. It is carved with an angel's face and blackened by smoke.

'Gorgeous, isn't it?' he says, his voice, an Irish-American burr, softening a little. 'We had a huge fire in a building in the East Village and these were every ten feet on the façade. They were all falling off, so I kept one.'

He smiles at it in silence for a moment and then he is off again. 'So when you get something like this breaking free and falling from a hundred feet it does a lot of damage to a soft body. So my only interest is public safety. It's not about the aesthetics or the preservation. It's not a problem with the wing nuts; it's not a problem with the paint job; it's not a problem with the occupancy. That's not what I do. When I get a building here in my shop it's because there's been a call or complaint about the structure. And the problem with physical structure is that once it starts to move, it's very difficult to convince that building not to move.'

You get the feeling that if a building were capable of listening to anyone, it would listen to Tim Lynch. In fact, he often talks about the built environment as if it were sentient in some way, describing how a failing building 'doesn't care' about your time frame, how it can 'seduce you' into thinking it is stable, how to understand it you have to mentally undress it, or, as Tim puts it, 'look at it in its underpants', how he has been 'chased out' of a disintegrating tenement that came down behind him, how (chillingly) a building on the verge of collapse will 'squeak' at you. This level of intimacy with the mien of failing buildings allows Tim and his team to assess with considerable reliability what is going to happen next and, more importantly, when.

'I'm anticipating all the time. If you're in reacting mode,' he says with a shrug, 'you're done, it's over.' And if you were in any doubt of the seriousness of what can happen when buildings fall down, Tim's conversation is peppered with mentions of a fatality here, a fatality there, presumably occasions when the call to the Buildings Department came too late or was never made.

'Look at how many reports we've got,' says Tim, moving on through the office and patting one of the hundreds of piles of paper. 'We do, like, twenty thousand of these every four or five years.' Asked whether this side of the job can be a bit dull, he says sharply, 'Absolutely not.'

For this is no bureaucratic backlog. Indeed, these paper-drifts of information are the key to how Timothy D. Lynch manages risk. The entirety of his decision-making in a potential or an evolving emergency – '*all of it*,' he says twice, patting the reports again – relies not upon instinct, or guess-work, but upon knowledge, and knowledge that comes from close study of all these records of failing bricks and mortar.

'You read so many of these things, you can see patterns,' he says, 'and a lot of what I do is looking for patterns. I've got 120,000 hours of experience over thirty years because I work 3,000 hours a year. And I never switch off. My mind thinks about this stuff, day and night. I dream buildings all night long and it never makes me not sleep. It's not a passion either, it's just my memory. I memorise everything.'

He pulls out a file of line drawings of sundry crumbling buildings. They are very detailed and rather beautiful.

'I do these. Quickly. When I get back from the site,' he says. 'Always from memory, never from photographs. And it's not that I have a brilliant recall for everything. It's just a memory for *this*. I can memorise shapes and I recollect details going back decades and decades. I see patterns instantly. Yeah, chasing patterns' – and he pauses, tracing a finger along a skewed roofline.

The point is that all that knowledge, all those patterns, have coalesced into lightning-quick risk wisdom, a decision-making ability so honed that it reads as a declaration of war upon any ideas, like Taleb's, about irreducible randomness. For, as Tim says, 'the real enemy here is not the building, it's time. We're chasing time constantly and we're chasing gravity.' Lines like this only add to Tim's

magus-like mystique. Some of his colleagues even murmur reverentially about how he has 'a sixth sense', but he swipes a hand through the air at the suggestion.

'It's not that. It's just a processing of this kind of data that's become very, very fast in my head. But it's not a guess or instinct. It's a calculated thing, an algorithm. I just do it very quickly.'

It may sound cold at times, but this knowledge and calculation have a practical, even a kindly, application. For they are, alongside Tim's feather-weight physique, what allow him to enter structures so frail that they would prove extremely hazardous to anyone else. He can, he says, simply calculate where the load is and pick his way around the danger. And this has given him a heroic aura in some quarters, known as he is for fetching people's life savings from condemned buildings, their heart

pills, their fish tanks, even the Torah scrolls from a crumbling synagogue.

'Is my job dangerous?' he says, looking at his watch and picking up a hard hat from the desk. 'The environment is horribly dangerous. But do I take risks personally? *No.* You just have to look at me. I'm wearing a uniform. I polish my shoes every day. I'm very conservative. I do nothing that makes my heart race.'

He grins, and that is as close as Mr Lynch is prepared to get to a disquisition on the nature of intuitive courage versus cold, hard reason. Besides, there is an emergency unfolding at this very moment up on 29th Street. The call came in last night, the emergency demolition order signed within hours, and Tim's site visit is in half an hour. 'Let's go,' he says, and he makes for the elevator.

* * *

As Tim drives across Manhattan from the Buildings Department on Broadway, up the Avenue of the Americas, through SoHo, skimming the West Village and the Flatiron District, he natters away about his job. He tells stories, such as the time he fell through a floor eight feet into a basement and straight onto a sofa that made him bounce back up again, to the hilarity of his colleagues; or how during Hurricane Sandy he and another engineer went to the top of a high-rise construction site to assess a crane that had blown over in the 80 mph wind and how they had to be tethered together to stop him blowing away; or the countless tales of failing buildings he has ushered into their grave, pointing out what he calls 'dentals', the gaps like missing teeth in smart streets where they once stood.

Because, in this city so full of hope and ambition, a monument to all that man can achieve in the name of a new beginning, Tim's currency is ephemerality and decay. For all his good humour and his practicality, the fragility underlying all human endeavour is pretty close to the surface in Tim's world, which may account for a certain steeliness in his character; this stuff could get you down if you let it.

'We do a lot that's kind of dark,' he says, 'but if you make a decision, everyone can move on.'

Knowledge and decision-making seem to be Tim's armour against risk, the heart of his skill at handling it. No Black Swans for him. Yes, the world may be filled with surprises, but much of what seems to be random may be marshalled by a tireless mind like that of Mr Lynch, or so it would seem. According to his philosophy, it can be contextualised, understood, even predicted. Tim's habit of asking questions and then answering them himself, immediately and decisively, is evidently not just a conversational tic but indicative of a deeply held worldview.

'I think people mistake risk,' he says, 'for not asking the right questions and looking for the answers.' And he parks the car on a smart Chelsea street, gets out and pulls a pair of steel toe-capped boots out of the trunk.

'You can ruin a pair of shoes in this job,' he says.

There on 29th Street amid some of the most prime real estate in the world is a nineteenth-century four-storey brownstone rowhouse. Through the broken glass of the upper panels in the front door, you can see it is completely derelict inside. Light switches hang on wires, the walls are blackened and patched with ply, a stained sofa cushion and a bag of cement sit at the bottom of a rotten staircase, the only sign of this building's former life a stout and gracefully curved wooden banister.

Tim steps inside gingerly. 'No, you stay there,' he says, and he disappears into the blackness, reappearing a short while later only to inch his way up a plank that has been laid up the side of the fragmented staircase into the floor above. In the direction he has just walked, towards the back of the building, you can see the glow of daylight where there should be walls. At length, Tim emerges onto the front step and says, 'It's very frail. Floors have gone, relieving walls, lots of them gone. There's

nothing locking it in on both sides and there's a wall at the back that's collapsed. It's a delicate demo job. It's not stable. Got to take some height and mass off the building. You do it by hand from the top down with cherry pickers, little by little. I'd start at the front, because I think if it rolls, it'll roll this direction.' He flicks his thumb back towards the sidewalk. 'And yes, we're going to start this today.'

The building's owner is standing by the front door.

'In the beginning,' he says, to no one in particular, 'we were thinking we were going to renovate it, but then—' He leaves the sentence unfinished.

Tim walks by him and says, 'Time to move on. It'll be gone in three days.' Then he adds, 'So that's that,' and he takes off his hard hat and heads back to the car.

6

Up in the air

An even more prolific coffee drinker than Timothy D. Lynch was the twinkly-eyed philosopher Voltaire -- upwards of fifty cups a day would arguably give anyone twinkly eyes – and rumours abound that *Candide*, his great critique of optimism in a risky world, was written during a single brief caffeinated frenzy. It was in his *Dictionnaire philosophique*, however, published five years later, that Voltaire wrote something that finds echoes amid the inevitably crumbling edifices of New York City. 'We are all formed of frailty and error,' he wrote. 'Let us pardon reciprocally each other's folly – that is the first law of nature.'

Now, on the whole, it is hard to fault a plea for tolerance, even one as pessimistic as this, for that is the context in which Voltaire's assertion is made. But home in for a moment, if you will, on the second of those weaknesses he mentions: error.

Error may be all very well in certain contexts. Everyone makes mistakes; we all know that. It is how we learn and grow, as the children of Plas Madoc's junk playground have shown. Moreover, in adult life, our little blunders stand testimony to our humanity, proof that we are not machines, vital signs of our capacity for change and invention. Yet there are some situations in which error simply cannot and will not be tolerated – indeed, in which even the chance of screwing up, however vanishingly slim, would be considered an aberration, the kind of risk that we should never, ever run.

Adrian Dolan's is one such world. Indeed, his is not a story about risk at all, so much as a story about risk aversion. And it is a risk aversion so nuanced, so finely honed and indeed so systematised, as to create one of the safest risk environments (or the riskiest safe environments) in the world.

★ ★ ★

Ady, as everyone calls him, is an air traffic controller at the busiest airport in the UK and the busiest dual-runway airport in the world, London Heathrow. Here an average of 1,350 planes take off and land every day, which in aviation rush hour can amount to up to a hundred planes an hour. In air traffic control terms, it is one of the top jobs, like playing first violin in the New York Philharmonic or striker for Chelsea FC.

Sitting at the foot of the 87-metre control tower in a bland, modern meeting room with a door of poster-paint green and a table of poster-paint blue, Ady Dolan cuts an affable, reliable figure, very clear, calm and, dare one say it, very controlled. He is exactly the sort of person you would wish to be ushering your holiday into the air or your business trip back down onto terra firma. He has an hour to talk before his shift begins upstairs and he carefully takes off a black digital watch and puts it

on the table in front of him. He has never worked anywhere else, nor wanted to. It is a job he loves. Passionate about aviation since his teens, he arrived straight from university fifteen years ago to train with NATS (National Air Traffic Services, which runs all air traffic control in the UK) and from training went directly into the high-volume, high-complexity environment of Heathrow.

As planes promenade to and fro beyond the plate-glass window, like grand old ladies being taken out for their Sunday walk, he explains how there is no obvious career path to becoming an air traffic controller. There is a rigorous vetting and training process, of course, with 3,000 applicants whittled down to just 20 every year, but they are a mixed bag. Among his team, he says, is someone who used to work in a call centre, another who has a first-class computer science degree. He himself studied geography and did summer jobs on the

check-in at Newcastle Airport. 'There is almost nothing to link us,' he says, 'apart from the specific aptitude for this task. You can either do it or you can't. It's just the way your brain is wired.'

This baseline aptitude seems to be comprised of decent spatial awareness, sound teamwork, an ability to digest multiple sources of information and, in Ady's words, 'come out with a really good decision within a very short space of time. That's what I enjoy,' he says, 'the instant problem-solving. There's not a great deal of prolonged thought about it. You just make a decision and then your decision happens in front of your very eyes. You see it unfold.' He pauses and glances out of the window, as a 747 rolls sedately past. 'It's rewarding.'

The way Ady says this makes it sound not exactly easy – because he also elaborates on the many months of theoretical study, the hundred hours in a 360-degree wrap-around simulator and many more in 'live' training – but certainly it is not a process that comes across as fraught in any way. In fact, the very reverse, chiefly because this is a system designed to be error-proof.

'You should never be putting anybody in a seat upstairs,' he says, 'and exposing them to some known risk that you're expecting them to just juggle and deal with by the seat of their pants. If we're crossing our fingers at any time, then we've definitely done something wrong.' And he laughs loudly, not because it is funny, but because, in his world, it is absurd.

In lieu of individual improvisation, there is intense collaborative vigilance of the sort that might foster nasty office politics in another setting, but which here is the key to how they handle risk. For the continuous assessment that marks the training process simply never stops.

'It doesn't matter if you are twenty years old and it's your first day,' says Ady, 'or you're fifty-eight and you've done forty years here, everybody's watching out for everybody else. So every three months for your whole career you sit down and talk about how things are going, any safety concerns you've got about a particular procedure or a colleague's performance, and I think once you get past that hurdle of why-is-everybody-watching-me, well, the reason they're doing it is because we're all obsessed with aviation safety. And you realise that actually it's quite right that it should be like that, and that it's like that right up until your last shift.'

This ethos of safety fixation is also formalised

in procedure. Ady spends a significant slice of his working life writing procedures, never by himself, of course, always in a team no smaller than three. Think of this as a combination of Dante's *Inferno* and a conference centre away-day: a process of summoning all your demons, studying them with fear and loathing, then neatly and methodically scoring each for their calamitous potential, and at length arriving at a polite, collegiate way of slaying them, every last one.

Ady puts it like this: 'There are so many safety management committees here, there are safety management committees for the safety management committees, and it's because we're obsessed with identifying risk and absolutely rooting it out of the system.' In the ordinary way, the word 'obsessed' comes with some whiff of the pejorative, unhealthy, unhinged, but not here. In air traffic control, obsession is good. 'Because,' Ady goes on, 'the only way you can run Heathrow with zero risk would be if you had only one flight a day. So you have to take an initial risk and mitigate it to within an inch of its life so that it ends up coming from here' – Ady waves a hand above his spiky haircut – 'right down to here' – his hand plummets to below the blue tabletop – 'so that if the risk did carry through to an outcome, it doesn't really matter, it's going to be such a non-event there'll be no effect, or the controller might have to make an extra telephone call or something.'

Now this is not a movie for which you would wish to attempt the elevator pitch, but if it is not white-knuckled entertainment you are after, but a smooth passage to Boston for that meeting, or to Nice for that week on the Med, then this level of risk aversion is just the ticket. Indeed, we airline passengers need people like Ady Dolan to do this, not just practically, but psychologically too. For there is no getting away from the fact that an airport is full of tractable human souls who, however thrusting and alpha in other parts of their lives, have temporarily surrendered all autonomy in the name of getting somewhere quite far away, quite fast. Meekly submitting to be corralled through a succession of security and retail pens, tranquillised by the (golden) opportunity to pay through the nose for a Toblerone the size of a crowbar, we are then packed into unfathomably high-tech toothpaste tubes to be fed microwaved ham rolls and very small cans of our favourite fizzy drink, as we are hurled through the air to our destination. This unqualified abnegation of responsibility for any risks that might be involved is a key part of the story here. Delegating the risk wisdom to professionals like Ady Dolan is part of what you buy when you buy a plane ticket. They do the thinking for us, so that we can study the in-flight magazine and try to block out the small child kicking the back of the seat.

Even taking into account tragedies, Black Swans indeed, such as 9/11 or more recently MH370 and its ill-starred cousin MH17, commercial air travel remains remarkably safe, outstandingly so compared with other modes of transport like driving, where we do more of the risk management ad hoc ourselves. Ady concedes that 'there will always be an element of risk', because something

happens that has 'never been seen before' – a pilot, say, puts the wrong information into his flight computer and turns left after taking off instead of turning right, it is a gusty day so it is hard to keep an aircraft on course, or, as happened only yesterday, says Ady, 'a big V formation of geese flew back and forth, back and forth, right in front of the tower. We had to stop everything for three or four minutes.'

But – and this is the risk that preoccupies air traffic controllers more than any other – what is at stake here is not life and limb, but what they call 'separation', that is to say the standard of a thousand vertical feet and three horizontal miles that must exist between any two airborne planes. It offers the ultimate example of a 'manufactured risk', to recall Beck and Giddens's ideas of the risk society. 'And that,' says Ady, 'is what you base your whole career on. We don't come into work every day trying to avoid a collision. For us that's just so many miles away. For us it's about ensuring that aircraft don't get within that separation standard. It's like putting a bubble around an aeroplane, and you don't want any aeroplane to go into someone else's bubble.'

This is a rare beast indeed: a margin for error so substantial and so sacrosanct as to make the error itself unthinkable. An air traffic controller's dominion may be up in the air, but there is precious little else in his world that is. That is the point.

In real terms, such obsessive mitigation of risk is a process that has been revolutionised by technology. Ady speculates that 'if you spin forward another fifteen years' many of the decisions he makes now will be made by machines. There is already a system in use based on an algorithm called Collaborative Decision Making, which times

and orders all flights pushing back from the gate in the safest and most expeditious way possible. 'The utopian dream,' says Ady, pressing imaginary buttons on the table in front of him, 'is that you just press go and all the aeroplanes just follow the plan. But we're not there yet, because there are humans involved, people turn up late to the gate, the catering truck breaks down, or the fuel doesn't get on the aeroplane, but that's what everybody's driving towards and we've started the journey. Still, to get to a position where there are no humans involved at all' – he looks out of the window at a man in a hi-vis jacket wheeling an industrial trolley across the concrete – 'I don't think that'll be in my career. I think the main thing is that as a passenger you like the idea of a human having some say in case something goes wrong.' And it is true; we need to feel that the management of anything that might jeopardise our well-being is in the hands of someone actually capable of caring about it.

This cocktail of all-too-personal human responsibility in combination with the culture of obsessive risk aversion could quickly turn you into a bag of nerves. So there is one last 'skill', as Ady puts it, that every good air traffic controller should have in abundance, and that is what he calls a 'massive, massive disconnect'. He says it again: 'Massive disconnect. Because people ask, *What's it like having all those thousands of lives in your hands?*, but we never, ever think like that. I was once out with another controller from here and someone said, *What is it that you do?* And he said, *I import and export aluminium tubes*. And that is pretty much what we do. Because if you started thinking, *Oh my God, what about all the children on board*, then would you operate as efficiently? I don't think so. So you have to block that stuff out. The way that we're thinking about it is that aeroplane is a 747 and it's going to Kennedy, it's on a Compton route so it's going to fly straight out of here via that point, it's going to fly initially at 250 knots, it's going to cruise at flight level 370 and I need to transfer to this particular sector. But that's it. It's just a big piece of aluminium.'

This is part of a broader process of divesting the day-to-day of all the variety that comes with a human face, of standardising every last communication into something that is neutral, error-proof. When Ady and his colleagues talk to the pilots, there is no 'Oh, hello. How are you? Off to New York, oooh, lovely. Weekend?' Ady laughs like a drain at this. 'It's weird in a way,' he says, still chuckling, 'because people actually say, *Oh, I was talking to a Lufthansa*, or *I was transmitting to an Air France*, they don't say *I was talking to the pilot of an Air France*. You actually talk to the aeroplane, and then the aeroplane responds. It's like you're talking to the machine as opposed to the human on board it.'

'Talking of which,' Ady smiles and picks up his watch from the table, 'better get up there.'

* * *

It is interesting (and perhaps no accident) that at no point in Ady Dolan's interview does he use the word 'accident'. This is not because it is some kind of taboo or act of denial. On the contrary, as we have seen, he is paid to give constant and close attention to what can go wrong. But perhaps it may be because his is a world in which things that Just Happen are kept to the bare minimum, unpredictability contained. In fact, the word 'accident' itself is derived from the Latin *accidere*, 'to happen, to fall out'. The word crops up in English in the Middle Ages now with an added inference of chance, 'a chance happening', and from there, a century or two farther on, seems to have acquired the negative overtones of not chance alone, but *mis*chance.

At any rate, accidents happen, do they not? And in the early 1980s, in the wake of the Three Mile Island nuclear meltdown, the eminent American sociologist Charles Perrow tried to work out why they happen and how. His focus was not the slips, trips or even the car crashes of everyday life, but large-scale, catastrophic systemic failures of complex technological systems. The theory that emerged cited the inherent flaws in tightly structured, intricate systems like the nuclear plant at Three Mile Island, and how a small, imperceptible failure, a tiny swerve, in one part of the system could cause an unforeseen cascade of other failures with disastrous consequences. Perrow's point was that this was no freak occurrence, but a fundamental design fault. It was, he said, 'normal', even inevitable.

Hugely influential though it is, Normal Accident Theory, as it is called, is nonetheless a pessimistic creed, a kind of twentieth-century high-tech spin on Voltaire's point about frailty and error. And so perhaps it was inevitable that before long someone (namely a small cabal of psychologists and political scientists at UC Berkeley) was moved to point out that perhaps the glass was not half empty, but half full. Not *all* high-risk technological systems are so lacking in resilience, ran their optimistic counterblast. In fact, they argued, there are some of them that are actually pretty good. Just look at the safety record of aircraft carriers! they cried. Or of air traffic control! Look at the thousands of gruesome disasters that could but do not happen every single day. And they set about formulating a theory of how these so-called High Reliability Organisations (HROs) function. These are organisations, just like Heathrow air traffic control, that rely on technology and complex processes and in which the risks if those technologies or processes were to fail are very high, so high in fact as to rule out

any option to hone the system by trial and error. Instead, they have to get it right every time. They have to be *reliable*.

Most fascinating is the study of what these HROs have in common in terms of their organisational character traits. Think of it as a kind of risk-oriented Seven Habits of Highly Reliable People. For all HROs have highly qualified staff and continuous training; they all have regular, reproach-free audits of performance within a working environment unhampered by pointless formality and hierarchy; they evince what one researcher calls 'collective mindfulness', they 'worry chronically' about what can go wrong and they feel a sense of shared and individual accountability for ensuring that it never does. They are, in short, one compelling version of what one might term 'risk wise'.

★ ★ ★

The lift journey up from ground level through the centre of the 84-metre steel mast and into the cab of the Heathrow control tower makes your ears pop. Then you emerge through the lift doors of poster-paint yellow and ascend the final flight of stairs to where Ady and another six controllers from C-watch are working in their high-tech aerial gold-fish bowl. The atmosphere is quiet and aquarium-calm. You can hear the soft footfall of shoes on the carpet, low voices murmured into headset micro-phones, the occasional pleasantry exchanged. Dotted here and there around the circular floor are large black industrial fans for hot days and the glass that encircles the space is lightly tinted, as in a diplo-matic vehicle. Controllers are dressed in jeans and T-shirts, a woman in a dress and cardie, an older man in a smartish blazer, another much younger in a hoodie with NYC written on the back. They sit in pairs, headsets plugged in, at long dark blue desks that bristle with screens, telephones, broad illuminated consoles that map the airport in grey and yellow, with little moving tabs marked UA47 or JAL43, BAW436 or AA51 in tidy replication of their roaring counterparts down on the sun-drenched tarmac below. On a raised dais in the middle of the room are the two air controllers, one running the southern runway where outgoing planes are taking off, the other the northern runway where incoming planes land. Everyone else is managing the 160 or so other planes down on the ground and Ady is supervising. A man in a jauntily checked shirt has just finished his shift. He slings a record bag over his shoulder and says to Ady, who is sitting tapping

virtual flight progress strips on a screen with the top of his black Bic pen, 'Is it a day to go and strim the grass in the garden? Or is it a day to go sit in the office?' Ady laughs and murmurs 'See ya' without taking his eyes off the airport below.

And out on the horizon you can see the grey smudge of central London, with its cardiogram skyline, and Windsor Castle to the north, beneath a cloudscape that would not look out of place in a baroque painting. The airport appears strangely miniature from this height, the grass geometrical shapes of green baize, tarmac like a chalky blackboard with orderly doodles of bright yellow lines that make pathways between terminal buildings criss-crossed with silvery ventilation ducts and gantries. The planes themselves look tactile from above, the light glossy on their backs. You feel you might like to pick one up and fly it through the air in front of your face. A tiny figure in orange hi-vis makes his way to a little blue tractor with a trailer full of grass and drives it over to his next mowing assignment. And in the sky the lights of approaching planes twinkle like stars even though it is early afternoon.

'See my point about the disconnect?' Ady says over his shoulder. 'It's like a kid's toy set, isn't it?'

And you cannot help but agree.

7

The law of gravity

'You make a mistake sometimes, you know?'

'Like what?'

'OK, here's one. August 2011. The time I ripped my face.'

'*You ripped your face?*'

'Yeah, I was skiing with Charlotte in New Zealand and I made just a split-second wrong decision. I thought I could get round a snowboarder. I reckoned I wasn't going to make it the way she'd gone, and I wasn't able to tell her to stop, so I just changed direction. And there was a rope rather than a panel of netting like you'd have at a normal ski resort. It caught my face, here on the left-hand side. It ripped my maxilla. It was disgusting. There was blood everywhere and Charlotte thought it was her fault and I thought I was dying. She was getting people to look through the bloody snow for my teeth.'

'Your teeth?'

'It turns out they were all there, they were just shoved forward so much that you couldn't tell. It was horrible. Anyway, you can't see it now because the maxillofacial surgeon was amazing.'

And Kelly Gallagher smiles, only the barest hint

of a shadow on the front of one of her beautiful, white, straight teeth.

* * *

Kelly is a professional alpine skier, her torn face just one of a catalogue of sporting injuries. A year after the episode with the rope and the bloodied snow, she was helicoptered off a mountain in Austria with a bruised spine and severe concussion.

'So there is a massive risk,' says Kelly in the blithe, chatty way she has of discussing any subject, whether it is a great night out or ripping your upper palate in half. Or, for that matter, backs broken on the snow; she lists them – 'there's Tim', 'Anna', 'Sean', 'Russell'. 'So I personally know four people whose whole life has changed. That's the risk. But there is an inherent joy you get from the actual skiing, and having found something that makes me happy, why wouldn't I then do lots of it? There's this thing we have about thinking less and living more. That's our whole motto in a way.'

This is not the kind of slogan that would cut it in air traffic control, but that does not mean it is ill conceived. On the contrary, thinking less and living more is key to Kelly's relationship with risk.

Sitting not far from her home in Bangor, County Down, overlooking the Belfast Lough and the green hills beyond, and working her way through a pot of herbal tea and a stack of tiny scones, Kelly is highly persuasive on how impossible High Reliability would be in her world, or even plain old Reliability. You find yourself not questioning her often idio-syncratic logic until long afterwards, partly because

of the speed and sheer quantity of her discourse, partly because of the earnest way her small pale hands garnished with nail polish the colour of ox blood stir the air, and chiefly because you sense it is all underpinned by a formidable resolve. One of the few people to whom Kelly willingly deferred was her much-loved father, an airline pilot who died in 2012. 'He was so wise,' she says, 'I would run everything past him.' But even the Gallagher pater-familias made no headway on this issue of personal risk. Indeed, the worlds of father and daughter, the institutional hyper-caution of commercial aviation and the life of a professional ski racer, could not have been farther apart.

'Me and my daddy used to have lots of conver-sations about this,' she says, swallowing a mouthful of scone and dabbing jam on another, 'because there's an envelope of limitations that goes along with aeroplanes but push beyond that and you know what's going to happen. That plane is going to stall; it's going to go into a spin. So he always used to say to me he couldn't understand why I would fall in certain races. He was like, *But why are you pushing yourself farther than you know you're able to go?* He'd say, *Every time I'm coming into land, I know exactly what type of landing it's going to be'* – Kelly leans forward and lowers her voice, clearly knowing she is about to say something heretical – 'and I used to always wonder was it just luck?' She laughs. 'But with sport compared to flying, skiing in particular, you are always, always pushing yourself. You leave nothing out there. You ski at the very edge of your control because anything less doesn't win.'

And if there is one thing you need to know about Kelly Gallagher, it is that she likes to win. The other thing worth pointing out is that she is registered blind.

Kelly was born with a genetic condition called oculocutaneous albinism, which affects the production of melanin in the eyes, skin and hair and which in Kelly's case means that she is severely visually impaired. She can see, in her words, 'not very much'. 'It's not like things are blurry,' she says, 'it's that there's just so much light, I can't make them out.' If she looks at a person or a place, she says, Kelly can just distinguish 'blocks of colour and that's essentially it'. It is not that her world is dark, but overpoweringly, dazzlingly, bright.

What this means on the slopes is that Kelly skis with a sighted guide, another ski racer, Charlotte Evans, who was there looking for teeth in the snow the day of the ripped face and with whom Kelly has skied for the last four years. Wearing a bright orange bib, Charlotte skis ahead and, connected by Bluetooth headset, Kelly follows the orange blob downhill at speeds of 100 kph and more. This sounds a good deal more straightforward than it is. For the velocity, the lines, the spacing all need to be constantly and minutely modulated at the same time as always push-push-pushing the overall speed. Moreover, the risks Kelly and Charlotte take must be taken together, no room here for the daring individualism that so often characterises extreme sport. Instead it is a complex relationship built upon reciprocal and highly defined responsibility, blistering honesty, continuous negotiation and renegotiation of ambition, trust, communication and a whole lot of practice too. All this is too intense to foster anything so tranquil as a friendship, but Kelly says, and she clearly means it, 'I really care about Charlotte. As a sister, you know?'

The longer you talk to Kelly Gallagher, the more you realise that her skiing career has not come about despite her blindness, but in many ways because of it. As a child, she attended a regular primary school in Bangor and describes how her teachers' solutions for dealing with her visual impairment were not those she would have chosen for herself.

'I wanted to go out and play with the other children whereas they did a risk assessment and decided that it wasn't best to let this little visually impaired girl with huge glasses on run around the playground and get knocked over. So I stayed in with the children who had an ear infection or something.

And I thought, *This is lame*. Because I didn't want to be different. So I think there's stuff that might not have been part of my personality had I not had bad eyesight. There were always things I wanted that I just had to find a way to do separately. And it was definitely the same with skiing.'

While her mindset was a lifetime in the making, skiing itself came about for Kelly almost by accident. She simply tried it one day on a family holiday when she was seventeen and was instantly hooked. When she went to university to read maths, holidays were spent on the ski slopes with her friends, who would make a little diamond formation around her to keep her safe. And she discovered she was fast too, very fast. Mentioning this still makes her smile from ear to ear. In 2007, she approached the British Disabled Ski Team and, the following year, they took her on. In 2009, she quit her civil service job, hired a full-time guide and, to everyone's surprise, not least her own, they were accepted for the 2010

British Paralympic team. It was, says Kelly, an ad hoc and 'pretty carefree' progression. 'It was just like, *Well, I'll have a go at this and see what happens.*' All the way along, there were naysayers, people who said this was not the way it was done, she was not good enough, too old, too inexperienced and the rest. 'But for me,' she says, 'it hadn't changed from the reason that I've ever tried anything in the first place. Maybe it was a closed door and I just decided I wanted to open it.'

In a telling reminder of the DOSPERT scale with its glimpses of the relationship between risk and values, this for Kelly Gallagher is where risk sits, every bit as much as in the concussions, the torn ligaments and broken backs. It lies in putting your dreams on the line, your dignity, in running the oh-so-painful risk of embarrassment, in teaching yourself to think less and live more.

'I guess you don't want to be labelled as a fool,' is how Kelly puts it. 'People might have thought I was foolish to think in 2009 that I could become a Paralympic champion. It *was* a foolish idea, you know, if you'd put the odds on it. Unless you really knew what I was willing to do, you wouldn't have been able to place a decent bet on it. But they' – she gestures to an ether full of detractors – 'they just don't know what you're willing to put into it, do they?'

In truth, the two sets of risks, physical and reputational, are intertwined here in a way that no tidy psychometric scale can ever quite capture. For in her account of the recovery from her physical injuries, in particular the severe concussion in 2012,

Kelly strongly echoes the sentiments of Dorothée Gilbert speaking of how a physical setback can awaken a whole world of mental jeopardy. 'You lose your confidence and confidence is something I've really struggled with. That's where I would say you take the biggest risk. You lose trust in yourself and then you start to think, *I don't want to be injured*, and also it's very real to us as visually impaired athletes, we compete with people who are in wheelchairs permanently so you think, *I don't want to hurt myself that way*. But mainly the risk or the fear is not even that. It's actually just a fear of failure.'

The pay-off for overcoming that fear is a mountain-top moment of euphoria – or rather a mountain-bottom one. This for Kelly is not about the adrenalin rush, which she says makes her feel sick, or even necessarily the speed; rather the feeling of control, of making the ski bend under you, 'making a bit of wood come alive and drive you down the slope, it's not sliding, it's carving, it's alive. That's the feeling you're chasing, that joy,' she says. Ask how much of achieving that is down to nerve and how much technique, she quickly replies, 'All of it is nerve, I reckon. The technique's already there.'

* * *

In May 1895, William James – the American philosopher, early psychologist and, as it happens, the novelist Henry James's elder brother – delivered a speech to the Young Men's Christian Association of Harvard University, where he was a professor. The address was provocatively entitled, or fittingly so, if one considers the angsts and existential hiccups that beset the student years, 'Is Life Worth Living?' The short answer, according to James, was 'yes', but the manner in which he arrived at this heartening conclusion affords an equally heartening perspective on the taking of risks.

Much of James's earlier thought had been given over to a search for the material functions of thoughts, not how they mirror or distort the truth, but what they *do*. Indeed, the meaning of thoughts, or so he argued, lies in their utility as handy tools for working out a) what to do and b) how to do it, like a kind of Swiss Army knife for the soul. On that count alone, the optimism that underpins many a leap of faith or risk taken proves uncommonly useful in an uncertain world, a world, as James put it, that is full of 'maybes':

  '*Not a victory is gained,*' said James to the assembled company, '*not a deed of faithfulness or courage*

is done, except upon a maybe … not a sally of gener-
osity, not a scientific exploration or experiment or text-
book, that may not be a mistake. It is only by risking
our persons from one hour to another that we live at all.
And often enough our faith beforehand in an uncertified
result is the only thing that makes the result come true …
Be not afraid of life. Believe that life is worth living, and
your belief will help create the fact.'

And so William James took the connection between risk and what we value and drove it to its natural conclusion: that an ability and indeed a willingness to take risks is fundamental to the well-lived life.

* * *

Today is Kelly Gallagher's first time in the gym for two months, since she and Charlotte won Britain's first ever Winter Paralympic gold at Sochi in 2014 and so began a whirl of sports celebrity appearances around the country. It is here at the Sports Institute Northern Ireland that the province's full-time professional athletes, Olympians and Paralympians, whip themselves into shape. Kelly usually trains full-time, five days a week, like a regular job, during the months she is not on snow in Europe, and the time has come to begin all that again. 'I've been eating for two months,' she says to the trainer, 'and, d'you know what? I don't feel guilty at all.' She has brought her medal to show everyone, a chunky disc of gold and glass, as heavy as a gym weight. 'The wee Queen's seen it,' she bubbles, 'and the President of Ireland.'

Outside the gym, of course, there remain

plenty of life's swerves that cannot be tamed either by training or by sheer force of character. A year and a half before Sochi, Kelly learned this cruel lesson in a way that has nothing to do with elite sport and everything to do with a rather more universal experience.

Shortly after her concussion on the Austrian mountain top in 2012, Kelly returned home to Northern Ireland to recover and regroup. While she was there, her father, who had successfully overcome a bout of eye cancer two years before, was told his cancer had returned. He was given a year to live, but lasted just six short weeks. For Kelly it was, and clearly still is, devastating.

'I was such a daddy's girl,' she says, 'I would have rather got cancer and died than him. But I've never seen somebody fight so hard being told that there was no hope. And I don't regret the fact that

he tried and totally failed. You know, that idea of risk and hope and putting everything you've got into things? I don't have a fear of it any more. Because I've seen that even if there's no hope, even if it's not working out how you want, you may as well throw everything you have at it and just keep going, because,' she makes a rare pause, 'sure, what else have you to do?'

It was this most brutal of lessons which Kelly cites as having driven her to win gold at Sochi. She and Charlotte had fared badly in the downhill race on the first day, coming last on the board and spending much of the afternoon in tears. The following day was the Super G, another speed event, and so Kelly says, 'I felt like it couldn't get any worse, so I was like *fuck it*, we may as well make the most of it. Because you can think of all the different scenarios and invariably it won't even turn out in any of the different permutations you've thought of. And maybe life's too short or it's too long to not take the chances you are given, because sometimes opportunities just go away from you. So we made a decision to just ski with no fear essentially. And we got our gold.'

She pauses. Then she says, as if in proof of William James's point about self-belief and her own about thinking less and living more, 'There. We were supposed to have a gold. Good.'

8

Possible futures

A few weeks after that day in the Belfast gym, Kelly Gallagher was awarded an MBE in the 2014 Queen's Birthday Honours List. Knighted the same day was the eminent statistician David Spiegelhalter. But his honour came not for taking risks, but for understanding them.

Professor for the Public Understanding of Risk at Cambridge University, David Spiegelhalter nevertheless expressed doubts about his inclusion in this book. In a kindly email to the author, he wondered whether he would not prove 'very dull' alongside 'people who have done real things with their lives'. Now for some, such may be the burden of a life spent in academe, but Spiegelhalter is no cerebral wallflower. It would take the whole of this book, in fact, to give a full account of his contribution to statistical methodology and its ramifications for the communication of risk in the wider world. Indeed, the sheer scope of Spiegelhalter's roving brief may be read as some indication of quite how extensively notions of risk and our burning need to marshal it has reached into every corner of our lives. A few choice career highlights include roles as lead statistician on the public inquiries into the Bristol children's heart scandal and the Harold Shipman murders; the development of now widely disseminated statistical software called WinBUGS, which produced as of the last decade the third-most-cited paper in all of mathematics and statistics; a prominent position in sundry expert advisory groups on everything from breast implant safety to volcanic ash clouds; oh yes, and more honorary doctorates and academic medals than you could shake a stick at, a Fellowship of the Royal Society, an OBE and now indeed a knight-hood, although this was still a secret when David Spiegelhalter agreed finally to meet, in spite of his 'very dull' disclaimer.

Besides, he is the opposite of dull, as he proved one drizzly morning in his book-filled office with its large blackboard of equations and graphs, its stacks of exam papers and empty coffee cups. Bouncy as a schoolboy, and every bit as irreverent – for this is one *éminence grise* not above a bit of swearing and the odd joke – David Spiegelhalter neverthe-less leaves you in no doubt as to his profound commitment to his vocation and to his particular brief in this professorship. It is telling that when asked about his proudest achievements Professor Sir David Spiegelhalter, OBE, FRS, offered the two following examples:

'I'm really proud to have become a public-oriented statistician,' he said, 'because in the past, they were grey-suited people, sitting in the back row, keeping quiet, and I don't think they should be. I regard risk and statistics as being the sharp end of maths in real life and I'll be proud if I've changed the environment in which numbers and stats are

discussed. But you know the thing I'm most proud of? My appearance on *Winter Wipeout*.' There was a little silence. 'You haven't seen my appearance on *Winter Wipeout*? Look, I'll show you. Because that was a real risk. I could have made a complete tit of myself, but it worked out well, very well.'

There followed a volley of laughter and the next two minutes was spent watching YouTube reruns of 'Professor Risk' in mortar board and gown running the obstacle-course gauntlet of nasty snowballs and swivelling spongy ski poles over a swimming pool of icy water.

'That's why I love getting older,' he said, still chuckling. 'Although I get more cautious physically, I get bolder socially and bolder in terms of taking reputational risks. When I get an honour or whatever, I think, *Great, this gives me the chance to do something more idiotic.*'

But there is a serious point to David's public profile, one that extends far beyond any game show.

Author of a popular blog, dozens of newspaper and magazine articles, documentaries and hundreds of public talks, he is downright evangelical about bringing statistics to the wider public. This is not simply enthusiasm for his own arcane academic discipline, but a fervent belief in the importance of educating people about how to read risk. Intelligent decisions, he argues, about everything from health and diet to politics and sex, depend upon it, while the gatekeepers of that risk information need steering towards more responsible, accessible reporting. In other words, What We Talk About When We Talk About Risk is not only part of risk itself but also of substantive importance in how we handle it.

That is because a recurrent dynamic of our relationship with risk lies in the mismatch between how we *should* make risk decisions (rationally, wisely) and how we *do* (instinctively, emotionally). There is a catalogue of biases and fallacies that come into play when we humans engage with uncertainty. And by the way, that includes the professors too, as David was keen to point out, citing how he also feels nervous when flying, or how he had worried with sixty-year-olds everywhere about whether or not to take statins to keep cholesterol down.

But David's core point was clear: that by using numbers, we can navigate the wash of sentiment that sweeps over us as we behold the abyss of what we do not, or cannot, know for sure (and nevertheless mind about tremendously). Numbers, in the form of probability, can offer a kind of life raft from which to make judgements about the tilt and swell of the unknown. To wit, acquiring some level of statistical literacy is absolutely central in his view to becoming risk wise. It is essential not only in working out what risks you should and should not take, but also in order to protect yourself against abuses of the *'lies, damned lies and statistics'* variety.

'I do think,' David said, opening his glasses and shutting them, quite solemn now, 'that numbers can influence your feelings, your emotional response, if you think about them carefully, and that's what I'm really interested in. And this is important because I think that ability to handle number and magnitude is vital to being an informed member of society, because otherwise people will manipulate you, not just politicians, but people trying to flog you stuff, banks trying to sell you insurance, charities, they're the worst, people trying to sell you opinion, newspapers. They'll say, *Oh, this is really dangerous*, or *Oh, don't you worry your little heads about it*. And you need to be able to critique that. It's part of being a basic citizen and that's what my job is for.'

Yet we 'consumers' of risk statistics, however well informed, however able to spot a ratio bias, or a positive from a negative frame, may remain vexed by how we are to understand our own individual relationship with the numbers in a statistic, such as 1 in 100 or 1 in 1,000. How can we reconcile their intrinsic plurality with our own fierce singularity? As Patrick McGoohan famously barked in *The Prisoner*, 'I am not a number! I am a free man!' Instinctively that is how we feel, and it tempts us to ignore a good statistic when we should be paying attention.

'This is really difficult,' said David apologetically. 'I can't give you a simple answer philosophically for how to go from this hundred people to *what does it mean to me?* But I do think there is a way around that I use for myself and that it's my life's ambition to get into popular discourse – and it is the idea of Possible Futures.' David turned around and, amid the Bayesian formulae and the graphs, started to draw lots of smiley faces and a few sad ones on his blackboard to denote desirable and undesirable future scenarios. 'The point is that these aren't all equally likely,' he went on, as he drew, 'and the trouble is that anxious people get obsessed about the worst that can happen' – David tapped at one of the miserable faces with his chalk – 'so the thing to do is to get them into perspective by realising there's lots more of these smiley ones. By the time you've gone through that, you don't need to weigh up anything else. And, actually, if there are a lot of those' – he turned and tapped the sad face again – 'then just don't do it. Or mitigate it.'

David turned back and smiled, his own face framed by frontiers of uncertainty in the form of a little throng of happy and sad faces behind him on the board.

'So it's only a metaphor,' he said. 'I mean, there's a zillion billion Possible Futures because every molecule and every atom is changing all the time, but that, for me, is what enables you to move from the population idea of statistics and a body of past events, to say something about your own future narrative, because that's what risk is. In the

past, things were rates, they're proportions. In the future they're risks and a judgement.'

And in those chalky faces, simultaneously cute and profound, one could suddenly see Lucretius's swerve and Nietzsche's living dangerously; Beck and Giddens's risk society and the DOSPERT scale; Taleb's Black Swans and the counterpoint of High Reliability models; even Voltaire's waspish

scepticism about 'the best of all possible worlds' and William James's noble leaps of faith. There they all were in the smiling and the sad faces on Professor David Spiegelhalter's blackboard.

* * *

The encounter that began with *Winter Wipeout* ended on a sombre note. Asked a question about which risk-takers he most respected, in spite of their contravention of the logic of happy and sad faces, David Spiegelhalter said something that opens up a whole new world beyond numbers alone:

'Those I most admire,' he said, 'are the Red Cross and Médecins Sans Frontières people who go into difficult situations, because their risk-taking is of so many different aspects in their work. It's both physical, the danger they're in, but also it is a massive emotional risk to expose yourself to suffering people. It's something that I don't want to do, I'm glad my kids aren't doing it because of the danger to your mind, the risk to your own psyche, of being a witness. The point is we tend to focus so much on mortal risk, you know, either gloom or smile' – he flicked a thumb back at the faces on the blackboard – 'but there's a huge amount in between. So I think those are the people I admire because someone's got to do it and it's more than risk-taking, isn't it?'

9

A life to save

An encounter with David Spiegelhalter can make one a little nervous of calling upon statistics to serve an editorial purpose, but wish me luck. For as risks go, according to figures from the Aid Worker Security Database, humanitarian work in Afghanistan at any point in the last five years has been the most dangerous on the planet.

Indeed, the number of major incidents of violence against aid workers recorded in the country between 2010 and 2012 – killings, kidnappings and serious injuries – is more than twice as many as in any other part in the world, and the overall global figures are steeply on the rise. Furthermore these figures do not include the non-violent threats, the data on which is thin compared with the more newsworthy data on violence, but which rank highly as risks within the humanitarian community; namely road traffic accidents (one of the foremost hazards in aid work), diseases or the mental health issues so starkly outlined by the Cambridge professor of risk.

All of which is to say that, in an already highly risky career, to undertake a mission in Afghanistan in recent years is, on paper at least, to fulfil the very etymology of the word 'risk' with all its inference of running into danger. Yet few would argue that this is not a risk worth taking. Indeed, it is of vital importance in the modern world. We need the humanitarian system to exercise our collective duty of compassion towards people themselves so intensely vulnerable to risk that without our help they may die. But that does not mean this is a job for everyone, least of all in the war-ravaged Afghan heartlands.

It is, however, the perfect job for Christian Schuh. A paediatric nurse from Witten in Germany, Christian works for the German Red Cross and has undertaken international missions in the Philippines after Typhoon Haiyan in 2013, in Haiti after the 2010 earthquake, in Zimbabwe during the 2008 cholera outbreak and for fourteen months between 2009 and 2011 as a paediatric nurse in a Red Cross-supported hospital in Kandahar in Afghanistan. Yet ask Christian if he thrives on risk-taking and he will look at you as if you have gone quite mad.

'I never,' he says, pausing to choose his words, 'put myself or my team into unnecessarily dangerous situations.'

'OK, but are you cautious by nature?'

'Yes.'

'And that's across the board?'

'I'm not impulsive if that's what you mean,' he says, looking down into a cup of black coffee he is holding with both hands, 'I was never bungee-jumping, you know?' – a glimmer of a smile passes over his face – 'No, I'm eighty per cent, maybe seventy per cent, mind-driven, so I'm always trying to think about the effects and side effects of things I'm doing. There are those grey risk decisions,

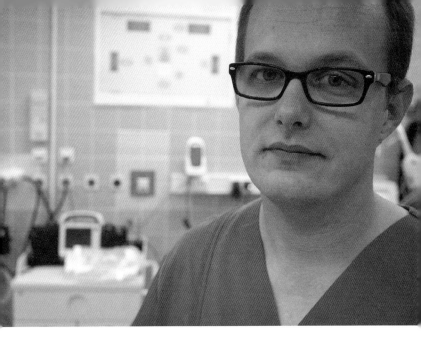

without any question. And then you have to discuss and decide how likely a negative impact is, how large the positive results might be, and then, in the end, it's a very lonely decision. But there are two different types of safe: a hundred per cent safety or ninety-five per cent. And that five per cent, if everybody agrees it's worth doing, then that's OK to buy the life of ten patients, or whatever.'

'Do you literally measure it like that in your mind?'

'No, but I do negotiate with myself,' Christian says, 'is this risk worth taking? And then I may decide, yes, but not' – he snaps his fingers – 'impulsively. I think about it. I'm stepping back in my mind to get a higher position just to oversee the situation, thinking for fifteen, thirty seconds, one minute, to make a plan. It's a rapid assessment, for sure, but it's not rushed.'

It is a fine example of Thinking Slow, to quote Daniel Kahneman's masterful characterisation of the two systems of our minds, System 1 or Thinking Fast, which runs on impulse, intuition, emotion, and System 2, which relies upon reflection, computation, choice. It could reasonably be argued (by the author's System 2) that a risk wise humanitarian aid worker, like Christian Schuh, requires a particularly well-tuned balance of these two systems, in order to weigh compassion on the one hand, that visceral urge to do good, with a particular ability to step back and Think Slow in situations so febrile that they would make most of us stop thinking at all.

Christian is based, between missions, in the German Red Cross regional office in Münster, but today he is at the national headquarters in Berlin preparing for a contingency planning meeting of the international Emergency Response Team in Washington, DC. Sitting in a strangely empty modern room next to a pristine red sofa and some bare Ikea bookshelves, a catering flask of coffee on the table in front of him, he talks of emergency and death, poverty and violence, chaos and war. His manner throughout is very careful, deliberate and a little deadpan, though never dispassionate, and you can see why; if your conversational currency so closely resembles the four horsemen of the apocalypse then there is little need for fervid embellishment.

As for the ability to Think Slow, it is a skill in Christian's case that is in part innate, insofar, as he says, as he is of a 'relatively calm' temperament, but it is also – and this should prove of comfort to anyone hoping to become better at handling risk themselves – something he has learned.

'In my early days fifteen years ago in the paramedic services,' he says, sipping his coffee, 'I started to learn this. And all those small pieces of practical experience help create this …' – he searches for the word – 'ability to deal with these things.'

Christian began working on a voluntary basis for the German Red Cross (which offers local welfare and emergency services across Germany) when he was eighteen years old, an alternative to the then compulsory national service.

'I didn't want to be part of the military,' he says, 'because I think it's much better to do good things than bad with weapons in your hands. And this was from my childhood. My friends were always playing cops and robbers with plastic guns and those were games I didn't like.'

After a social sciences degree at university, the thought of an office job filled Christian with gloom, so he moved instead to full-time paramedic training and from there into paediatric nursing. The transition reveals an intriguing modus operandi. It was because, so he says, 'in the paramedic services you are always afraid of being the one responsible for very small children or newborns in difficult situations. I was always thinking, *Let's hope I don't need to do this.*' It is a telling window on Christian's particular response to anxiety and difficulty that he simply decided to learn how to do it. 'I needed for myself to feel more secure in that kind of emergency environment,' he says. Three years later, just

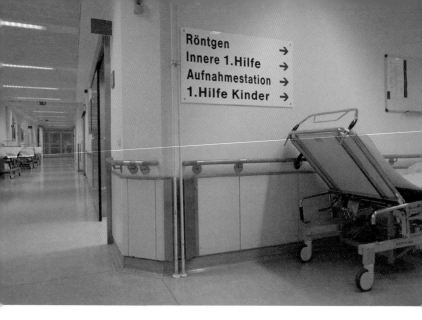

before his 24th birthday, he began work in neonatal intensive care.

A stream of fascinating insights follow from one of the most extreme hospital environments in the developed world. He speaks of how intense it is both emotionally and technically to work with new lives as fragile as these 500- or 600-gram babies; how the positives and the negatives become accentuated, the happy moments ecstatically so, the sad hugely difficult; how you become a conduit for all the parents' hopes and fears; and how the psychological resilience to do this work comes with a combination of disposition and of practice.

'You have to be able to protect yourself, or to be protected,' he says, tracing his finger on the tabletop as though drawing a diagram. 'You always have to be self-reflective but you also have to be able to share and discuss those things and not to just take it home or ignore it. So, you step back for some

minutes, some hours, some days, if necessary. You
have small breaks, you get out of the situation with
a cigarette, with a coffee, maybe with a newspaper,
or if it's a really tense situation, then this break can
be longer and you have colleagues around you who
will substitute for you before you reach the point of
being overwhelmed. This is how it has to work, and
it always worked in my experience.'

Despite the seeming mismatch, this has much
in common with the High Reliability mode of
managing personnel, as used in air traffic control.
In Christian's case, it afforded him a sound lesson in
managing psychological risk, one that would serve
him well in situations too chaotic and too dire to
permit any such formal emotional cordon sanitaire.
For alongside his hospital day job, Christian had
begun to take various International Committee of
the Red Cross (ICRC) courses in disaster response,
water purification, emergency sanitation, security
training and so on. His first emergency deployment came in 2008 with the cholera outbreak in
Zimbabwe. It was, he says, 'interesting', 'compelling' and 'very different', but it was the call he
received three months after he returned home,
early in 2009, which was to lead to a life-changing
mission.

This was the opportunity to deploy as a
paediatric nurse to the intensive care unit of the
ICRC-supported Mirwais Hospital in Kandahar in
Afghanistan, not for the usual six-week emergency
response, but for six months.

'So I thought about it,' he says, 'and then I said,
Yes, why not?'

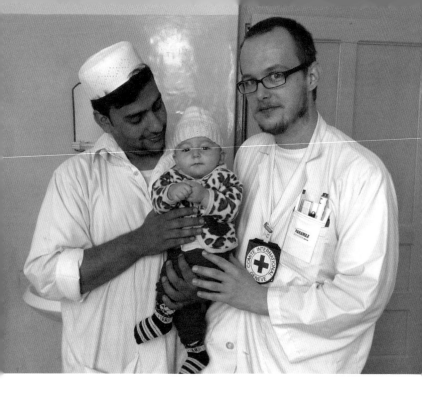

A few vaccinations, some additional security training and Christian found himself some weeks later in one of the hottest spots in southern Afghanistan in one of the hottest years of the war there. He had never been in a war zone before and here he was treating the injured Afghan policeman one minute, the next the Taliban insurgent's daughter. In this potentially explosive situation, Christian learned quickly the unique risk-mitigating power of those intersecting red arms, 'the protective sign', as he calls it. He tugs at the red canvas waistcoat on the back of his chair: 'Wearing one of these, always,' he says. 'Red crosses on the cars, on your shirt, on your baseball cap, always. Because you are not a target. Everyone wants the Red Cross or Red

Crescent doing this work, but to be in the middle of a city like this in the middle of a war zone, that's dangerous.'

There are established ICRC drills on the safest conduct under such circumstances, all geared to not being, as Christian puts it, 'in the wrong place at the wrong time'. In practical terms, this is less about flak jackets and helmets and more about not walking anywhere, even the 500-metre journey between compound and hospital, no shopping centres or markets, every journey festooned with Red Cross flags, strategically planned and announced with absolute transparency as part of the close regular contact with both sides in the conflict. But the drills afford you only a measure of security.

'Being there was scary in the beginning,' says Christian. 'You'd hear an explosion five kilometres away and you knew, *OK, this means in fifteen minutes, ten patients are coming*. But, after a few weeks, large explosions, AK-47 Kalashnikov machine-gun fire, it became a daily reality and doesn't cause adrenalin peaks any more. Maybe only some unexpected thing does, an explosion two or three hundred metres away or thirty injured patients coming after a bomb blast. Then, for sure, this is a stressful situation. My colleagues would say that, from the outside, I seemed calm, though my insides—' and Christian mimes a churning motion with his hands. 'But I was able not to show this and to focus, as though through a tunnel, on the medical things.'

For all Christian's economy with the psycho-narrative of his work, all his low-key, measured,

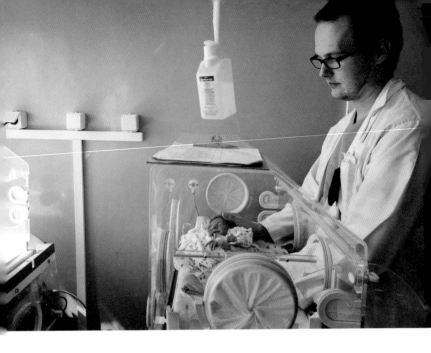

practical accounts of how to balance risk in a situation as precarious as war-torn Kandahar, the story he tells when asked about his hardest case speaks volumes. Here is no explosion, no gunfire, no insurgent threat, just a heartbreaking window on the reality of war.

During the first of Christian's two six-month deployments, there was a little boy aged two or three who came regularly to Mirwais. He was suffering from hydrocephalus or water on the brain, but there was no option to pursue the expensive shunt surgery that would be standard in such a case in Europe. Nevertheless the little boy, whom we shall call Yacoub, would come every four weeks for observation and some treatment of his symptoms. He was, says Christian, who met Yacoub on one of his very first days in Kandahar, 'a very polite, nice and bright child, just with a really, really large head'. But one day, after Christian had been in Afghanistan for about five months, Yacoub's family simply brought him for his appointment and were never seen again.

'They just left him behind,' says Christian. 'They disappeared without him.'

There is a long silence, then he takes a breath and says, 'So from a technical point of view, this was very difficult as we already have other children to take care of and it is very resource-consuming, but also, it was really, really sad. There's no system in this war zone to take children into care. You just need to find other families to take the responsibility and for this little boy, nobody wanted to take the responsibility. So we just kept him in the hospital.'

Yacoub was there when Christian left Kandahar at the end of March 2010 and he was still there when he returned for his second deployment that September.

'He was just part of the paediatric ward and then in the middle of 2011 he died because of his condition. But to leave a child behind, this was ...' Christian holds a steady gaze without finishing his sentence.

'From a practical point of view, I have some understanding for it, but ...' Again Christian does not finish and almost imperceptibly he shakes his head. 'It's war.'

Then he shifts in the shiny office chair and says, 'Could we have a three-minute break for a cigarette?'

* * *

Some have argued that contemporary ethical philosophy has not overly troubled itself with questions of risk in the real-world sense. Instead it has concentrated upon generating finite and often fantastical thought experiments to tease out specific ethical dilemmas, a world of runaway trolley cars that may either kill one man or six, or of experience machines that can offer us, if we so choose, a life of unmitigated pleasure and no pain.

Yet in reality, we all live lives full of uncertainties, both large and small, and where risk lies not neatly laid out in binary choices, but in the very fabric of our relationship with the future, all its fears and all its hopes. Both our sense of jeopardy and our astonishing resourcefulness in the face of it, as the encounters with the risk wise people in this book have shown, are an intrinsic part of being human. This is our natural state. And if we can only come to appreciate some of the manifold ways in which human beings have come not to master risk but to live well alongside it, then we too may become a little more risk wise ourselves.

So perhaps classical ethical thought can be more helpful here. As Seneca wrote, 'the really good man is not dragged by Fortune, but keeps pace with it'. Or as Aristotle argued of *eudaimonia* (that is, happiness or flourishing), 'it stands in need of good things from outside'. In other words, the well-lived life not only dances hand in hand with conditions of risk, but is also in part created by them.

And what could offer a better example of that than the story of Christian Schuh? Five months later, in November 2014, he would agree to join the Red Cross fight against the Ebola epidemic in west Africa, declared by the World Health Organization to be 'the most severe acute health emergency in modern times.'

* * *

Christian Schuh is now driving across Berlin bound for a large warehouse out by the airport, the logistics hub for all German Red Cross missions. He has his seat belt tightly fastened and his sat-nav primed in a van that bleeps when he reverses and glides effortlessly over the speed bumps on the leafy roads near Red Cross HQ. You cannot help noticing how very safe it all feels.

Out at the warehouse, all is order and preparedness. Here on ceiling-high metal racks sit pallets of tents, bales of blankets, huge yellow generators and industrial fans. There are steel cases of surgical instruments and power tools, wooden crates marked 'water purification', large balloon lights on tall, spindly tripods, grey corrugated plastic showers and latrines, white plastic washbasins with carbolic soap hung on hairy string and already in place. Towards the rear are parked dozens of jeeps and pick-up trucks, a few articulated lorries and several ambulances. There is enough equipment here, Christian says, for five or six emergency response units, each with a large field hospital, a base camp, water purification facilities and smaller healthcare clinics.

The whole place could not be a clearer statement of a certain relationship with risk, one that lies in being prepared for the worst and in having a plan for what to do if it happens. The other side reveals the human face of risk wisdom and it lies in something Christian said earlier, not long after the conversation about Yacoub.

'In Germany,' he said, 'we do the best for each and every individual with more or less unlimited resources, but in Afghanistan you had to decide to do the best for the most. Here in Europe it's very rare that children die in hospital, but there, on that ward, children were dying every day. This is difficult to learn to accept and it took me many, many weeks. But, when you have accepted this – and the local staff, the Afghan colleagues, they have – then you not only see the two or three patients who are dying every day. You see, more prominently, the 147 for whom you are doing good. So the perspective changes. I think you have to accept that there are some things you cannot change.' Christian leant forward and pushed his coffee aside as if to make room for his core point. 'And I try to focus on the things that *can* be changed, the good that can be done. Because that is something you can build on. Yes, why not?'

Conclusion

Alain de Botton

This has been a book about what makes us a little too cautious for our own good, an attempt to identify a golden mean between recklessness on the one hand and timidity on the other.

It's a book for our times, because now, more than ever, we are forgetting the role that intelligent risk has to play in every human advance. Paradoxically, it's because we have made the modern world so safe, so technologically predictable, so comparatively wealthy, that our risk-taking muscles have grown weak from under-use and we stand in danger of decadence, of forgetting what was required to secure our present advantages – and of running away from genuine opportunities. An age obsessed by safety has opened up a collective new danger: the sclerosis that comes from putting security above all other virtues.

The book is the result of an innovative partnership between Allianz Global Investors and The School of Life, who invited writer and film-maker Polly Morland to act as their Writer-in-Residence – a residency less about an author residing in a particular location than about residing within a specific *idea* or *concept*.

During Morland's residency, she explored a specific question: *in a world where risk is inevitable, how is it possible to embrace it wisely?*

We are social creatures, and when we think what level of risk might be 'normal' and acceptable, we look around and pick up suggestions. That's one of the good things about this book. Morland has not profiled the usual suspects. There are no Niagara Falls divers, English Channel swimmers, space explorers or sky's-the-limit entrepreneurs. The very scale of the risks taken by famous daredevils may put the rest of us off, breeding an unwarranted sense that the choice is only between deep caution on the one hand and what looks strikingly like sheer recklessness on the other. It isn't; the real world is full of very ordinary people who have taken what – to the world – will look like minor risks, but are in fact – to them – huge steps on a journey towards their own evolution. Perhaps they are letting their children play in a slightly unguarded way (Chapter 1), maybe they are living in a somewhat dangerous part of the world (Chapter 2), perhaps their job brings with it a slightly higher-than-average share of responsibility (Chapter 5).

Morland quotes Nietzsche's advice that we learn to 'make our homes on the slopes of Mount Vesuvius!' He first spotted a marked decline in attitudes towards risk in the nineteenth-century European bourgeoisie – and was bothered by it, for he took his own inspiration from the Ancient Greeks and Romans, those exemplars who took humanity to heights unsurpassed for a millennium. In his energising, bombastic, exhilarating prose, this is what the concept of risk and return sounds like:

> Examine the lives of the best and most fruitful people and peoples and ask yourselves whether a tree that is supposed to grow to a proud height can dispense with bad weather and storms; whether misfortune and external resistance … do not belong among the favourable conditions without which any great growth … is scarcely possible … What if pleasure and displeasure were so tied together that whoever wanted to have as much as possible of one must also have as much as possible of the other … you have the choice: either as little displeasure as possible, painlessness in brief … or as much displeasure as possible as the price for the growth of an abundance of subtle pleasures and joys that have rarely been relished yet. If you decide for the former and desire to diminish and lower the level of human pain, you also have to diminish and lower the level of their capacity for joy.

Indeed, the most fulfilling human projects appear inseparable from a degree of danger and torment, the sources of our greatest joys lying awkwardly close to those of our greatest challenges. We must strive to correct the belief that fulfilment must come easily or not at all, a belief ruinous in its effects, for it may lead us to withdraw prematurely from challenges that might have been overcome if only we had been prepared for the suffering legitimately demanded by almost everything valuable.

What can make us risk wise? It runs as a sub-theme of this book, but is worth spelling out directly: the thought of our eventual demise. It is only by reminding ourselves that the ultimate risk has already been written into the contract of life that we can stop being so precious about our own safety. We can loosen ourselves from an unhelpful sense that we can ever be safe by meditating on the ever-present risks to our existence. Indeed, the only real danger is regret; an eventual sense that we did not risk enough. It would help if more of us went into old people's homes and asked the simple question: 'What do you feel sorry you never tried?' The answers would frighten us, indeed terrify us into action – for what is scarier, from the vantage point of great age, than a novel not written, a person not kissed, a business not started. Hence the importance of those visualisation exercises, much rehearsed at business schools and on company away-days, when we are asked to picture our deathbed scene or our funerals and focus on what, from that perspective, will really matter. Was it really so important to please one's acquaintances and keep the boat steady? Why did one not have the courage of one's intuitions?

In medieval times, a normal piece of interior decoration for a merchant was a memento mori or skull, which would sit on your desk, not to remind you that everything was meaningless, but to bring your real priorities back into mind. Vivid reminders of mortality can put our prosaic obsession with safety into question. When measured against our limited time spans, the true insignificance of some of our concerns is emphasised and our narcissistic, frivolous tendencies can cede to our more sincere and purposeful sides.

If life is as fragile as it clearly is, if we really have no guarantee that there are decades left ahead, then we don't want to be that person who spent an afternoon arguing with a beloved, who refused to forgive a friend for a minor transgression or who neglected a genuine talent in favour of an unhappy sinecure. The thought of the end of our lives has the power to rearrange our priorities, returning to the surface the more valuable parts of us which have a tendency to become submerged in everyday struggles. Evidence of what there is really to fear can scare us into leading our lives as we know, in the core of our being, that we properly should.

A philosopher who appreciated this better than others, and can therefore help us with our fears about risk, is Martin Heidegger. He proposed that we rarely risk enough for ourselves because we don't live enough for ourselves. We surrender to a socialised, sanitised, superficial mode of being he called 'they-self' (as opposed to 'our-selves'). We follow The Chatter ('*das Gerede*'), which we hear about in the newspapers, on TV and in the large cities Heidegger hated to spend time in.

What will help us to pull away from the 'they-self' is an appropriately intense focus on our own upcoming death. It's only when we realise that other people cannot save us from death – what he termed '*das Nichts*' – that we're likely to stop living for them; to stop worrying so much about what others think, and to cease giving up the lion's share of our lives and energies to impress people who never really liked us in the first place. 'Angst' about 'The Nothing', though uncomfortable, can save us: awareness of our '*Sein-zum-Tode*' (our 'Being-toward-death') is the road to a more authentic life. When, in a lecture in 1961, Heidegger was asked how we might recover authenticity and live more fully, he replied tersely that we should simply aim to spend more time 'in graveyards'.

One of the most fascinating discoveries in Morland's book is that people's appetite for risk depends ultimately on one thing: how fervently they believe in something more important than themselves. The great risk-takers take risks because they live lives and have goals they fervently care about, more than they care about the traditional benefits of safety (a long life, money, comfort). From this perspective, the young writer who risks security for art isn't just being 'heroic' – the thought won't even have crossed his mind; he merely loves the craft of literature very much and lets this dominate his choices. Similarly, the chef who remortgages her house to launch a restaurant isn't blind to the theoretical benefits of safety; she just loves the business of cooking so much more. And the parent who steps in to save their child does so not because they themselves want to die, but because they want another (small) person to live so very much more.

This raises a new and discomfiting thought: perhaps the perceived decline in risk-taking is about a decline in the number of goals we feel we can sincerely believe in. We no longer want to sacrifice ourselves for religion or for the nation. We feel the danger of risking everything for 'posterity' when there might be no such thing. Yet that cannot be the whole story; there must remain what philosophers call 'transcendental goals', things more important than the individual. Being safe is of course a delightful thing, but there are ultimately many things that are better than it, better sometimes even than one's own life: such as one's children, one's family, one's vocation, the well-being of one's community. When one discovers a true vocation, one also discovers an indifference to pain. That's when the possibility of self-sacrifice comes to seem less galling. And that, in the end, is the message of this book: when one unearths one's true beliefs, risking a lot for them is no longer a risk. It's just what one has to do.

Everyone has a different image of what they would do, if only they were not so afraid. It might be leaving one's partner, it might be asking a friend out on a date, it might be starting a new enterprise, or betting one's money on a scientific development. The answer will always be particular, but the fears are invariably universal. As Heidegger knew, we should not ponder what to do next in the comfort of our homes. We should not weigh up risks in our cosy cocoons. We should put our lives into the perspective of looking backwards at the end of our lives. From this viewpoint, everything seems so much clearer – the benefits of risk are starker, and ambition and selfless courage are that little bit easier to locate within us.

Afterword

Why should an investment manager support a book about risk, in particular a book that looks at risk in everyday life, outside the financial sector?

Dealing with risk – managing it and harnessing it according to clients' needs – is at the heart of what an investment manager does. Risk per se is neither good nor bad; rather it is an expression of probability – the likelihood of a particular outcome, positive or negative. By definition, the professional investor takes risks in the capital markets every day – to buy, to sell or, indeed, to hold. The successful investment manager is a successful risk-taker, someone who sustains a record of good decisions.

Risk is not confined to the world of finance, of course; a society or an economy without it is unimaginable. It's something we all face daily, whether consciously or otherwise. And yet, in everyday usage, the word 'risk' has become laden with negative overtones. Indeed, when we speak of risk, it conjures notions of anxiety, hazard, even fear. In turn, profound risk aversion becomes a habit, one that can undermine good decision-making, tainting our institutional and social mores as well as our individual actions, and wider public discourse.

Studies of risk are nothing new. Disciplines ranging from sociology and psychology through to behavioural finance have all produced significant insights into how human beings confront risk and uncertainty. But sometimes a purely theoretical approach can feel remote from our ordinary day-to-day experiences.

Working with The School of Life, Allianz Global Investors wanted to explore what might help us to reconnect intellectually and emotionally with the concept of risk. We invited Polly Morland to take up an artistic residency, not within a particular physical space, but within a real world of everyday risks and rewards. The result is this series of compelling and engaging human stories which help us to reflect on the nature of risk from a variety of fresh perspectives and to explore what it means to be truly risk wise. This book is an inspiring journey, one that reminds us how learning to walk wisely hand in hand with risk can be positive and enabling.

Each of us is a risk-taker, and we have the capacity to become more risk wise as we learn to hone and trust our judgements.

We hope that this book will spark a rich public dialogue and open up new conversations about the meaning and role of risk in a fulfilled life.

Elizabeth Corley and Andreas Utermann
Co-Heads of Allianz Global Investors

Further reading

What follows here is not a reading list on risk. That would run to many pages indeed. Instead, here is a selection of the sources that inspired or informed this book and which may be of interest to those keen to read around and beyond some of the ideas raised in these pages.

Nicomachean Ethics, Aristotle, translated by J. A. K. Thomson (Penguin, 2004)

'Europe's ticking time bomb', Katherine Barnes (*Nature* 473, 2011)

Risk Society: Towards a New Modernity, Ulrich Beck (Sage, 1992)

The Norm Chronicles, Michael Blastland and David Spiegelhalter (Profile Books, 2013)

The Consolations of Philosophy, Alain de Botton (Penguin, 2000)

Risk: A Very Short Introduction, Baruch Fischhoff and John Kadvany (Oxford University Press, 2011)

Extremely Loud and Incredibly Close, Jonathan Safran Foer (Penguin, 2006)

Virtues and Vices and Other Essays in Moral Philosophy, Philippa Foot (Clarendon Press, 2002)

Runaway World, Anthony Giddens (Profile Books, 2002)

BBC Reith Lectures, Lecture 2, Hong Kong, 1999, Anthony Giddens

No Fear: Growing Up in a Risk Averse Society, Tim Gill (Calouste Gulbenkian Foundation, 2007)

'The median isn't the message', Stephen Jay Gould (*Discover*, June 1985)

The Swerve: How the Renaissance Began, Stephen Greenblatt (Vintage, 2012)

The Ethics of Risk: Ethical Analysis in an Uncertain World, Sven Ove Hansson (Palgrave Macmillan, 2013)

The Odyssey, Homer, translated by E. V. Rieu (Penguin, 2003)

Evolutionary Playwork, Bob Hughes (Routledge, 2011)

Is Life Worth Living?, William James, 1895 (can be read online at https://archive.org/details/islifeworthlivinoojameuoft)

Thinking, Fast and Slow, Daniel Kahneman (Penguin, 2011)

The Nature of Things, Lucretius, translated by Alicia Stallings (Penguin, 2007)

After Virtue, Alasdair MacIntyre (Bloomsbury, 2007)

The Gay Science, Friedrich Nietzsche, translated by Walter Kaufmann (Random House, 1991)

The Fragility of Goodness: Luck and Ethics in Greek Tragedy and Philosophy, Martha C. Nussbaum (Cambridge University Press, 2001)

Normal Accidents: Living with High Risk Technologies, Charles Perrow (Basic Books, 1984)

The Letters of the Younger Pliny, translated by Betty Radice (Penguin, 2003)

Ethical Theory: An Anthology, ed. Russ Shafer-Landau (Wiley-Blackwell, 2012)

On Providence, Seneca, translated by Aubrey Stewart, 1900, pdf http://en.wikisource.org/wiki/Of_Providence

The Black Swan: The Impact of the Highly Improbable, Nassim Nicholas Taleb (Penguin, 2008)

The Philosophical Dictionary, Voltaire, translated by H. I. Woolf (Knopf, New York, 1924)

Candide, or Optimism, Voltaire, translated by Theo Cuffe (Penguin, 2006)

'A domain-specific risk-attitude scale: measuring risk perceptions and risk behaviours', E. U. Weber, A-R. Blais and N. Betz (*J. Behav. Dec. Making* 15, 2002)

'A Domain-specific Risk-taking (DOSPERT) scale for adult populations', A-R. Blais and E. U. Weber (*Judgement and Decision Making* 1, 2006)

'The self-designing high-reliability organization: aircraft carrier flight operations at sea', G. I. Rochlin, T. R. La Porte and K. H. Roberts (*Naval College Review*, 1987)

'Collective mind in organisations: heedful interrelating on flight decks', K. E. Weick and K. H. Roberts (*Administrative Science Quarterly*, 1993)

http://understandinguncertainty.org/ is produced by the Winton Programme for the Public Understanding of Risk, based at the Statistical Laboratory, University of Cambridge.

The Aid Worker Security Database is a project of Humanitarian Outcomes and can be found at https://aidworkersecurity.org/

The German Red Cross can be found at http://www.drk.de/ and the International Red Cross at http://www.icrc.org/eng/

Acknowledgements

I am thankful to a great many people for helping to make this book happen. Above all, I would like to thank those whose stories feature here for their time, honesty and insight. It has been a privilege and a joy to spend the last few months in their company; as it has been to work and travel alongside photographer Richard Baker.

Heartfelt thanks to the team at Profile Books: Andrew Franklin, Paul Forty, Pete Dyer, Steve Panton, Anna-Marie Fitzgerald, Olu Ubadike, Ian Paten and, above all, my superb editor, Clare Grist Taylor; also to The School of Life's Ewen Haldane for bringing me on board in the first place, and to Alain de Botton for his fine conclusion. To Allianz Global Investors, in particular Marc Savani, John Wallace, Elizabeth Corley and Andreas Utermann, I am greatly indebted for their support of the project and for the freedom they afforded me to pursue this fascinating subject wherever it led.

I also want to thank the following people, who have helped in many ways, editorially and practically, at home and abroad: Dinah Bornat, Marion Cole, Nadine D'Austin, Kent Diebolt, Sandra Down, Lucy Edwards, Tim Gill, Lois Harris, John Hooper, Katherine Jackman, Colin Kennedy, Tania Kotlorz, David Laisini, Will Longe, Patrick

Macartney, Kelly Magee, Flavia Manini, Francesca Marascalchi, Emma Parry, Emma Piesse, Cath Prisk, James Rundell, Sarah Rundell, Nina Schöberl, Karina Shaw, Delia Shumway, Anne Smyth, Bernard Spiegel, Edward Thornton, James Walker, Helene Wallace, Patrick Walsh, Katy Whelan, Kevin Whelan.

Henry has, as ever, kept me sane, well read and well fed, while Sam, Milo and Freddie have inspired me with their own risk wise antics high in the trees outside my study window.

Polly Morland